Lydia Becker
and The Cause

Audrey Kelly

Centre for North-West Regional Studies
University of Lancaster

1992

For my daughters-in-law, Lyn and Sue

This volume is the twenty-sixth in a series published by the Centre for North-West Regional Studies at the University of Lancaster. Details of other titles in the series which are available may be found at the back of this volume.

ISSN 0308–4310

Published by the Centre for North-West Regional Studies, University of Lancaster

Typeset in 10/12 Times by Carnegie Publishing Ltd., Maynard Street, Preston
Printed and bound in the UK by Cambridge University Press, Cambridge

First Edition, 1992

British Library Cataloguing-in-Publication Data
A CIP catalogue record for this book is available from the British Library

ISBN 0–901800–13–9

Table of Contents

Acknowledgements

I would like to thank David Doughan and staff at the Fawcett Library, City of London Polytechnic, Jean Ayton, archivist and David Taylor, local history librarian, Manchester Central Library, the staff at Bristol Central Reference Library and Richard Violet and staff, Bradford on Avon Library for their assistance in tracking down and making available much of the source material for this biography, and Janet Harris who so kindly provided me with a base in Manchester during my research. Extracts from documents in the Manchester archives are used with the permission of the City of Manchester Leisure Services Committee.

Preface

AMONG my most treasured possessions is an eleventh edition set of the *Encyclopaedia Britannica*, an historic edition, published in 1911, the last truly British *Britannica*, copyright of 'the chancellor, master and scholars of the University of Cambridge'. Idling through the final volume, Vetch to Zymotic Diseases, I was surprised to find Women accorded a fourteen column entry and amused that the anonymous writer, presumably a man (only 7 out of the 204 named contributors were women), should believe that, by 1910, women's ability 'to take their place, independent of any question of sex, in the work of the world' had been satisfactorily resolved. The parliamentary franchise was glossed over, almost as an irrelevance, because 'with or without the possession of the vote on their own account' women were able to play a sufficient role in political life through such organisations as the Primrose League or the Women's Liberal Federation. The writer went on to summarise the women's suffrage movement and referred in passing to 'the earliest outstanding figure . . . Lydia Ernestine Becker (1827–90)'.

Here was a name that meant nothing at all to me, yet I was struck by the coincidence that Lydia had been born exactly one hundred years before me and that I was discovering her in the centenary year of her death. The bibliography led me on to Helen Blackburn's *Record of Women's Suffrage*, published in 1902, which I was delighted to find contained a biographical sketch of Lydia Becker whom the writer had known personally. There followed a visit to the Fawcett Library in London where, hidden away in a box of miscellaneous papers relating to her political activities, I unearthed and gently fingered a lock of Lydia's thick black hair, a spray of pressed forgetmenots and some diary notes recording 'don't like Tebbuts Tea as well as Brooke Bond' and 'sad accident to a basket of strawberries which fell off the top of an omnibus'. As I read on through this diary of 1873 where Lydia's formidable programme of speaking engagements stood side by side with 'badly cooked dinner' and 'scarlet runners black with frost', the outwardly austere and supercompetent political activist began to assume a human face and I even discerned certain parallels with my own life some ten years previously when I had struggled to reconcile the demands of family life with lobbying, campaigning and public speaking on behalf of the peace movement. I knew exactly what it was like, the constant weary round of meetings and petitions, the apparent lack of progress, the stigma of being labelled an activist and troublemaker. It was comforting to be able to relate to this woman who had been through it all exactly one hundred years before to pave the way for the political freedom I now enjoy. I had stumbled upon an undeservedly neglected figure and determined to share my discovery.

Introduction

IN an age that takes universal suffrage for granted the struggle to gain women the vote is associated almost exclusively with the suffragettes whose dramatic campaigning style, leading to arrest, imprisonment and hunger strikes has become one of the legends of history. The suffragettes may have stolen the limelight and secured themselves a place in the history books but the struggle had begun much earlier; a forgotten army of women was in the field some fifty years or more before Mrs Pankhurst became a household name, fighting for their right, not only to the franchise, but to a place among men in all walks of life. Lydia Becker was undoubtedly their chief of staff and, in the latter half of the nineteenth century, it was her inspired leadership which gave direction to the infant movement, which worked the change upon public opinion and prepared the ground for the final onslaught of the militants in the Edwardian era. Year after year she ensured that women's suffrage was kept high on the political agenda, she was the organising genius at the centre of a tireless campaign to overcome years of prejudice and win over the hearts and minds of ordinary people. Bills to 'remove the electoral disabilities of women' were regularly laid before Parliament throughout her period of activity and the Members of Parliament who introduced them were supported by petitions bearing the signatures of thousands of women – and many men too – and an orchestrated programme of public meetings, parliamentary lobbying and press coverage. It was never Lydia Becker's style to bring herself into conflict with the law; hers was the art of gentle persuasion as she worked quietly and assiduously to change the whole climate of opinion towards women, painstakingly preparing the ground for the activists who were to follow after.

The early stirrings of feminism and demand for the vote clearly pre-date both the suffragettes of the early twentieth century and the strong working class movement of the 1890s and coincide more nearly with the succession of Victoria to the throne in 1837. Not that Victoria had any sympathy with 'this mad, wicked folly of women's rights with all its attendant horrors' as she wrote in a letter to Sir Theodore Martin,[1] and if the early suffragists hoped that the accession of a young woman to the throne would further their cause, they were to be bitterly disappointed and disillusioned. Victoria seemed perfectly content to regard her own position as God-given and unique and offered absolutely no encouragement to her female subjects, many of whom were becoming increasingly restless and discontented in their purely domestic role with its limited horizons and felt that they wanted to make a more useful and active contribution to society. The Anti-Corn Law League, like the Chartist organisations before it, had encouraged women to help with their fund raising activities, welcoming their assistance at social gatherings, fetes and bazaars, but they were not allowed to take part in the discussions or debates. Yet it was only natural that their presence at such functions, if only to dispense tea and cakes, should awaken in them an interest in the issues for which their husbands were campaigning and would ultimately lead to a demand to be more directly involved.

By the middle of the nineteenth century women had begun to assert themselves. There was a great upsurge in all kinds of philanthropic activity, people were forming themselves into a multitude of groups and societies to promote one good cause or another, and women demanded a degree of participation in these new organisations. There was considerable male prejudice to

1

be overcome but, very gradually, women came to be accepted into membership on the same terms as men. The most enlightened of these societies was the National Association for the Promotion of Social Science, founded in 1857, and it was at a meeting of this association in Manchester in 1866 that Lydia Becker first came into contact with the suffrage campaign. She immediately threw herself heart and soul into The Cause, as it was affectionately known to its supporters, campaigning tirelessly for the next twenty-four years, co-ordinating the movement nationwide, establishing the first periodical devoted exclusively to women's suffrage and remaining the movement's most ardent and indefatigable champion until her death in 1890.

Plate 1. Lydia Becker, a portrait by Isabel Dacre.

Manchester City Art Gallery

Chapter 1

LYDIA ERNESTINE BECKER was born in Cooper Street in central Manchester on 24th February 1827, the eldest of fifteen children. She looked upon herself as a typical Lancashire lass and always remained fiercely loyal to her native city and county yet her family roots were in Germany and her paternal grandfather had come to England at the turn of the century, probably less than thirty years before her birth.

Ernest Hannibal Becker was born in Thuringia in 1771 but was driven from the country by the threat of conscription and, like other prominent manufacturing chemists such as the Mond and Brunner[2] families, he came to England to set up in business. Taking advantage of the industrial revolution in northern Britain he lost no time in establishing a flourishing vitriol works which supplied the Lancashire cotton industry and, about 1800, he took a lease of Foxdenton Hall at Chadderton which remained the family home for about eighty years. Little is known of Ernest Hannibal although he had the reputation of being a fine violinist and a brilliant linguist. He was also a great lover of the countryside and, for his day, a remarkable conservationist. On discovering that the manufacture of vitriol was injurious to the trees which, in a well wooded part of the country surrounded his works, he lost no time in re-siting the factory elsewhere. Foxdenton Hall had previously been the home of the Radclyffe family but the last member of that family to live there had neglected it badly and Ernest Becker was faced with the challenge of a huge programme of restoration and renovation. The house was in such an advanced state of decay that at first he lived in solitude and in great discomfort in only two rooms, but all the time he was working hard to build up and expand his chemical works and all the profits were plough-ed into the restoration of house and gardens.

Within a relatively short space of time he had made the house into a comfortable and welcoming home and he embellished the grounds with colourful floral displays, fine trees, splendid kitchen gardens and an aviary. One of the chief glories of the flower borders at Fox-denton was the collection of stocks, one variety of which was introduced into the neighbourhood by Ernest Becker and he named it after the well known politician John Bright.[3] It was said that the bloom had a distinctive colour and was as prominent among flowers as Bright among politicians, a sentiment which reflected Becker's own radical sympathies which, in turn, were to be carried on by his first granddaughter.

On 19th June 1800 Ernest Becker married Lydia Kay Leigh, nine years his junior, in Manchester Cathedral. They lived all their lives at Foxdenton Hall and their eight children were all born there. There were two sons and six daughters of whom at least one died in infancy. Lydia's father, Hannibal Leigh Becker, was the elder son born in 1803 and her uncle John Leigh arrived eight years later. When Ernest died on 29th May 1852 his younger son John took over Foxdenton Hall and lived there for another thirty years becoming a well known local figure both as a county magistrate and hunting man.

Hannibal worked for his father in the chemical business and at the age of twenty-three he married into an old Lancashire mill-owning family in Hollingwood who traced their origins back to the reign of Henry VI when an ancestor had been High Sheriff of Cheshire. Mary Duncuft was not yet nineteen when she married Hannibal Becker in March 1826 and it appears that they began their married life in Manchester because this is where their eldest child was born the following year. They named her Lydia Ernestine after her grandparents. Hannibal's father had given him the sum of £600 to build himself a house near the family chemical works at Altham near Accrington and, when Lydia was still a very young child, they moved into this large and pleasant property which they called Moorside. It was situated on rising ground with a fine view of Pendle Hill and it was in this beautiful country home that Lydia spent most of her early life. There was a brief interval during which the family moved to Reddish on the south-eastern outskirts of Manchester where Hannibal had acquired a calico printing works, but after a year or so they returned to Altham.

Mary Becker's life was dominated by a constant succession of pregnancies and, although she was fond of her eldest daughter, Lydia was left very much to her own devices and, from the age of about seven or eight, she was already taking some responsibility for the younger children. Two of her sisters, Bertha and Sofia, died as babies when Lydia was no more than six years old but she was closely attached to Esther who was born in 1834 and in later life Essie, as she was called by the family, wrote affectionately of their relationship and acknowledged that Lydia's influence upon her had been very great and that she owed much of her intellectual development to her. Essie lived to a great age and after Lydia's death she compiled a handwritten notebook[4] of reminiscences 'so that the children of the family may know something of her, and be proud to think they are of the same stock'. She was the only member of the family to support Lydia in her political activities; she made donations to her sister's suffrage society, she sold tickets for meetings, she cut out press cuttings from the local papers and sent them to influential people.

From an early age Lydia showed every sign of exceptional intelligence. Before she was two years old she knew all the letters of the alphabet and could name the animals in her picture book. By the age of five she was an avid reader with her head constantly in a book. She was a quiet and undemonstrative child but she absorbed knowledge like a sponge and took a keen and intelligent interest in everything around her.

Living uneventfully in a fairly isolated rural spot the children were thrown back upon their own resources and into close contact with each other, especially as they were educated almost entirely at home. For a brief spell Lydia was sent away to boarding school at Everton in Liverpool, but for the greater part of her childhood she remained at home, reading everything that came her way and being largely responsible for the education of the younger children. She taught them to read and to develop their powers of observation. Esther recalled in her notebook that 'as a teacher her powers were remarkable; she seemed to go right down to the bottom of things. It all came out so clear in one's mind'. Not only was Lydia a great reader, she had the gift of remembering everything she read and a wonderful knack of extracting the salient points from any book very quickly, which was to be of immense advantage to her later in her political work when she was deluged with parliamentary papers, bills and reports. She became a walking encyclopaedia for her younger brothers and sisters and was their universal point of reference whenever a particular piece of information was required.

Lydia never enjoyed particularly good health and she suffered from a chronic weakness in her back which was never completely eradicated. Esther once referred to a weakness in her hands and fingers which prevented her from mastering the piano and this same arthritic problem was apparent in her handwriting which had a peculiar unfinished look from her inability to grasp a pen properly and which sometimes made her writing extremely difficult to decipher, particularly if she was writing under pressure when legibility was obviously sacrificed to speed. Lydia was meticulous in her habits and it was a matter of great frustration to her in the offices of the suffrage society that she was unable to fold a circular neatly, because she feared that this might give the wrong impression to the public of a slipshod organisation.

In 1844, when Lydia was seventeen, Hannibal Becker sent his daughter to Germany in search of a cure and she spent a long stay in the beautiful surroundings of the Thuringian forest

Plate 2. A sketch made by Lydia Becker while on holiday in Germany. The caption reads 'this is just to give you some idea of the Schloss as it appears from my bedroom window; you must remember I cannot draw'.

where her father's cousin, Hermann Piutti, ran one of the many hydropathic establishments which were so popular with the Victorians. Her absence from home was keenly felt by the younger children; Esther was only ten when her elder sister went away and she recalled the occasion as a great event, a landmark in their quiet lives. Throughout her stay in Germany Lydia was a prolific correspondent and the letters which she sent home at regular and frequent intervals became a detailed chronicle of her visit. The journey itself was long and sometimes tedious. Her first letter home describes how she left Antwerp by train very early in the morning on Sunday 14th July and travelled all day to Cologne. She wrote rapturously of Cologne Cathedral, 'I never imagined anything so magnificent . . . I could never tire of looking at it'. From Cologne she travelled by boat down the Rhine, picking out the famous castles and the Lorelei rock which she said she had no difficulty in recognising, and seventeen hours later she disembarked at Mayen to complete the journey by coach. This was the most trying and wearisome part of the journey and there was one stage, near Fulda, when it took the coach fourteen hours to cover sixty miles, including stops, as much of the journey was steeply uphill. Lydia wrote that she had enjoyed sitting on top

of the coach although there was the constant danger of being struck by the tall overhanging trees which lined both sides of the road but eventually 'a Frenchman who had placed himself next me began to make himself disagreeable squeezing my hand' and she asked to change places with a gentleman riding inside. The complete journey had taken a fortnight and she arrived at her destination on 26th July.

Her written descriptions were frequently accompanied by little pencil sketches. There was one of a typical German castle with the note 'This is just to give you some idea of the schloss as it appears from my bedroom window, you must remember I cannot draw'. Her days were taken up with the strict regime at the Kurhaus where she went every day to take the recuperative mineral waters and she was also taking regular German lessons from the village pastor. There is no doubt that she benefited from the waters and the change of air. At Christmas she revelled in the thick snow and could write humorously of being tipped out of an overturned sledge and add 'I think I was never so well in health as I am at present'. Her German relatives enjoyed her company and Dr. Piutti wrote to Hannibal on 28th February 1845 to report on Lydia's progress:

I ought to have written to you and your dear wife long ago and to have expressed my gratitude for the friendship you have shown and the pleasure you have caused to me and my wife in confiding your dear Lydia to our care for some time. She is, I am happy to say, very much improved in health and vigour; a weakness in the back, which doubtless existed for some years, and having rendered her weak and unable to use her bodily strength, seems much better, thought not quite subsided. Lydia is grown tall and stout, and you will be quite surprised to see what a lady-like figure she will be when you meet her again. She is fond of learning and of everything that touches mental faculties and clever understanding; she is sharp and keen in her intellect, clever in judging matters, fond of knowledge, has an excellent memory, and her passion for reading facilitates the study of the German language at present very much, as she is now so far advanced as to read books in German easily. All that is mechanical gives her more trouble to do, although whenever she does it she does it well, viz., writing in German.

She plays sometimes on the piano very nicely and agreeably, though I think the weakness of her back will for the present prevent that practice which is wanted to carry it on to a higher degree of ability. She began drawing and painting flowers upon china and did it remarkably well. We sometimes have a game of chess, in which I am frequently the loser.

Lydia is the best tempered girl I ever saw, which principally and partly arises from her activity of mind, which is always busy, time never hanging heavy on her hands. She is always interested for things around her and does all she can to increase her knowledge of things.

Before she leaves Germany, which I trust will be a long while yet, I hope she will see Leipzig, Dresden, and perhaps Berlin.

Always yours most sincerely, Herman Piutti.[5]

A year later Lydia set out for home. Although she said goodbye to the Piuttis in July 1845 the return trip was to be a leisurely sightseeing tour and she did not reach England until late September. She was accompanied by her uncle John Leigh who had been sent to the continent to meet her; the weather was very stormy and they had an exceptionally rough crossing, passing dangerously close to the Goodwin Sands. At the time of her homecoming the family were living at Redditch. Young Esther remembered being much impressed on being reunited with her grown-up sister. Lydia had acquired a traditional South German travelling cloak of a style unknown in England, of heavy grey cloth and very long and distinctive. She had matured and put on weight and to her younger brothers and sisters she seemed a different person. The family kindled a great bonfire to celebrate her return and Lydia soon settled back into the domestic routine of the Becker household and began to teach her brothers and sisters to speak German.

Although Lydia was always conscious of her responsibilities as the eldest child and discharged her domestic duties with the utmost conscientiousness, as she grew into adulthood her lively mind needed more intellectual stimulus and she began to take an intelligent interest in politics and current affairs. In 1848 she began a journal in which she commented upon political events of the day. On 16th February she wrote:

> Lord Morpeth has introduced another Health of Towns bill into the House of Commons. I hope and trust he will carry it though many members object that it does not go far enough, that there is no mention in it of the wicked window tax, or of interment in towns.

In a later entry she was scathing about a debate in the Upper House:

> On Friday last the House of Lords, in their splendid hall with all the pomp of state that ancient descent and noble birth can give, sat gravely discussing the relative rights of hares and rabbits. Truly the regard for game is something very like superstition. Suppose all

the game in England were annihilated I am at a loss to understand what dreadful consequences would ensue.

The Becker children conducted heated discussions on current affairs among themselves, no doubt egged on by Lydia's strong opinions so forthrightly expressed and Esther recalled the excitement they felt when it was thought that the Chartists might find their way into their peaceful valley and also, in 1848, when Louis Phillipe[6] landed in England. She remembered their stormy discussions on the Anti-Corn Law League and, although she found the arguments somewhat unintelligible, she bowed to Lydia's more expert opinions which she attributed to her quick intellect and more advanced age.

The awakening of political consciousness went hand in hand with a deep and serious interest in natural science. In 1850 the family left Redditch and moved back to Moorside at Altham and the spectacular scenery of the neighbourhood encouraged Lydia's interest. She joined a class for water colour painting and, although she always depreciated her own efforts, she made some very beautiful sketches from nature. She took an intense interest in botany and scoured the countryside for specimens which were new to her. Her discoveries gave her immense pleasure, whether it was a *primula farinosa* on Pendle Hill or a rare sort of geranium in Symonstone Lane. She had an interesting correspondence with Charles Darwin[7] in connection with some facts she had observed in the course of her studies and she used to send him specimens she had found.

In 1862 she won the gold medal of the Horticultural Society for the best collection of wild plants made within a year. She had devised a method of drying plants very quickly under great pressure and in heat, using a press made of transverse pieces of wood which allowed the air to pass through, and using bricks covered in brown paper as weights. Her method preserved the original colour of the flowers and she mounted her specimens on paper using gum tragacanth so that no ugly strips would disfigure them.

In 1864 she published a little book *Botany for Novices: a short outline of the natural system of the classification of plants*. It was an attempt to explain the principles of the natural system of classification adopted by modern botanists to readers who had no previous experience of botanical science. The botanical terms are carefully explained and there are small, clear, engraved illustrations on many pages reminiscent of the pen and ink drawings in her notebook of 1848. Her own view expressed in the book is that

> . . . in nature, nothing is trivial or unimportant, the smallest and most ephemeral of beings owes its origins to the working of the same laws, and the force of the same Power that produces the greatest and mightiest on earth.

It was sad that this clear and explicit little book never achieved a wide circulation because it was written with all the directness and clarity which were later the hallmark of her political speeches and writings. Lydia's love of nature was well known to all her friends and one of them wrote that 'Lydia knew and loved every flower that grew'. She herself said that, had she not become embroiled in the suffrage movement, she would have devoted her life to the study of natural sciences and she always regretted that, as a woman, she was denied the university education enjoyed by her brothers. A fellow suffragist, Jessie Boucherett[8], said that Lydia's ideal of happiness was a small house in the country, a garden and a donkey chair. All her knowledge of flowers was based upon keen observation; if out for a drive she would constantly enumerate the different plants and flowers which she identified in the hedgerows as she passed. When her political activities took her to London her office was always brightened by flowering plants and her chief recreation was to refresh herself among the gardens and conservatories at Kew.

Astronomy had the next largest share of her studies in the pre-suffrage days and she prepared a companion volume to *Botany for Novices*, a little book on elementary astronomy which she called *Stargazing for Novices*. It was to be 'a simply description of such appearances in the sky as may be observed and understood by the unlearned who have no telescope'. In seeking to share her enthusiasm for amateur astronomy she wrote in the introduction:

> Everyone loves the stars. Everyone, on lifting his eyes to the glorious vault of heaven, feels the beauty, the grandeur and the mystery which surrounds these eternally fixed yet ever living sparkling orbs.

Although the manuscript is preserved and shows her thorough grasp of a difficult subject and her descriptive powers, she suffered the disappointment that it was never accepted for publication.

Chapter 2

IN February 1855 the happy, united family was devastated by the death of their mother from pneumonia. Weakened by twenty-eight years of constant childbearing, Mary Becker died at the early age of forty-seven. Lydia was desolated by the loss of her 'dearest mama' whose death left a void which she said could never be filled, and the situation at home was made more difficult by the strained relationship which had always existed between Lydia and her father who did not share her progressive views. Once, while in Germany, she had written regretfully to him that 'there has been little of the confidence of friends between us, but I hope this separation may be the means of bringing us nearer together'. A bereft husband and a grieving daughter now had to come to terms with each other and with a changed domestic regime and Lydia must have viewed her prospects with considerable trepidation. A conflict of emotions raged within her; on the one hand she longed to pursue and develop her intellectual and scientific interests, but on the other hand she was thoroughly domesticated and knew where her filial duties lay. Eleven of Mary's fifteen children had survived and chief responsibility for the running of the household now devolved upon Lydia as the eldest although she had the support of Mary, Esther, Ernest and Victoria who were all adults. Three of the other children were in their teens, but Wilfred was only five, Charles four and baby Louisa a mere five months old. There must have been a time of difficult readjustment when Lydia realised that, at the age of twenty-seven, she would have to devote her energies to her younger siblings, acting as mother substitute, housekeeper and governess, but she gave herself willingly to the challenging task and a friend was struck by the close and affectionate sympathy which bound the family together. In his later years even Hannibal was moved to speak well of his eldest daughter's domestic efforts, confessing that all the good in his children they derived from their mother. Lydia gave herself conscientiously to her domestic duties and it gave her considerable satisfaction to apply her scientific principles to every household activity, from supervising the laundry to making jam. A young relative who on some occasion was praised for her excellent dancing declared 'Ah, who do you think taught me, why Lydia; from a spring-waltz to a plum pudding I would back Lydia against any woman in England'. Even when she was fully committed to political activity she always kept a sewing machine in her room and was often to be seen cutting out and stitching garments for the family before taking up her pen to draft her next lecture.

The years following Mary Becker's death brought continuous tragedy into the family. On New Year's Day 1857 Lydia's dearly loved brother Ernest died in tragic circumstances in Brazil. He was only twenty-one and the shock of his death was so terrible a trial to Lydia that she could never bear any reference to it in the years to come. Although destined to remain a spinster, she was devoted to babies and young children and derived immense pleasure from her nephews and nieces, the children of her married sisters Mary and Victoria, and it was a bitter blow to the family when four of these little ones died in infancy. Her brother John Leigh had trained as a doctor and emigrated to Queensland, Australia which he described to his sister as a 'god-forgotten country' and, because he was not particularly robust, she worried constantly about his health and wrote him compelling letters urging him not to over-tax himself. Their correspondence meant much to her because she felt able to confide in him all her hopes and fears, and it grieved her most deeply to learn of his premature death on the far side of the world at the age of thirty-two. In the face of such constant tragedy she looked more and more to her unmarried sister Esther for friendship and support and she found pleasure and satisfaction in the successful careers of her surviving brothers, Arthur and Wilfred. Arthur won a scholarship to New College, Oxford, and studied mathematics and natural science before taking up a teaching post at Clifton College and later at Charterhouse. He was a brilliant musician and chess player and was said to have been one of the first to climb the Matterhorn from the Italian side.

In 1865, with the youngest child now eleven years old and two of his other daughters married, Hannibal Becker decided to give up Moorside and to move his much reduced family into central Manchester and he took a house in Grove Street. Despite her affinity with nature and her deep love of the countryside, the change in environment was a lifeline to Lydia, she rejoiced in the stir of human life she found all around her in a lively and prosperous city, and she was stimulated by the cultural and intellectual activities which were now at her disposal. She and Esther went to the theatre, to Hallé concerts and the opera and the family were regular supporters of the so-called Gentleman's Concerts in Manchester. On one occasion Lydia recorded in the family diary that Esther had returned from a fruitless errand to secure second class places for Don Giovanni, having discovered that tickets were not for sale in advance, but the day was redeemed when Lydia, browsing among the second-hand bookshops, found a copy of Schiller's *Wallenstein*[10] which she purchased for one shilling. But one aspect of Manchester's cultural life distressed and angered her – in a city which boasted so many societies for the advancement of science, none opened its doors to women – and she spoke out bitterly against the harsh and arbitrary exclusiveness of such organisations. She longed to bring more interest into the dull routine of women's lives and to encourage them to realise that there was more to life than domestic drudgery, so she started a little society for women for the study of scientific subjects and called it the Manchester Ladies Literary Society with herself as president. The Royal Institution in Mosley Street allowed her free use of a room for her meetings and several eminent men were persuaded to come and read papers. It was a brave venture and in her inaugural address she expressed the hope that her society would become a meeting place for instruction and discussion and a sympathetic exchange of views. She told her audience:

> Some persons may be tempted to smile at the idea of a number of ladies, whom they cannot suppose to be very learned, occupying their minds with such subjects as the Origin of Species or the Antiquity of Man . . .

> The implied censure would be well deserved were our professed object to throw any new light on these difficult questions, but as we meet simply to inform ourselves on what has been discovered and propounded respecting them, the reproach of ignorance cannot be justly employed as an argument to dissuade us from endeavouring to gain information. We believe there is no method so effective of fixing in the mind the information that is imparted to us, as that of a discussion, in which everyone is invited to ask any question that occurs, or to state unreservedly any opinion, along with the grounds on which it is entertained. We therefore determine to institute and encourage such discussions, and if the result should be, to prove to ourselves that we know very little of what we are talking about, that will surely be the best of reasons for trying to remedy the defect as fast as we can.[11]

The Society got away to an auspicious start with a good number of members and adequate funds to acquire a small library and Charles Darwin himself was persuaded by Lydia to lend prestige to the inaugural meeting by sending a paper which was read to the audience, but the success of the society was short-lived and it was a great disappointment to Lydia that it did not survive. Perhaps she set too lofty a tone in her speech of introduction, or perhaps she overestimated the enthusiasm of her members who, once the initial novelty of a society specifically for women had worn off, may have felt over-awed by the unaccustomed atmosphere of free-ranging discussion and debate. Or maybe it was her own inability to nurture her brainchild and give it her undivided attention once the suffrage movement had claimed her loyalty that caused it to fill.

It was at the very same time as Lydia was developing her scientific interests and trying to establish her Ladies Literary Society that she was suddenly brought face to face with the women's suffrage movement. It was a subject which had not crossed her horizon until, one memorable day in October 1866, she attended a meeting of the National Association for the Promotion of Social Science. This organisation, then in the ninth year of its existence, had become the centre and mainspring of the humanitarian movement and it was remarkable for its time in that, from the very first, women were welcomed and admitted into full membership. They attended meetings, submitted papers, and even more unusually, were allowed to read their own papers before an audience, take part in discussions and be admitted to public dinners. The success of the National Association and the fact that women were allowed a role within it on equal terms with men was an immense encouragement to public spirited women. For the first time they had a forum where they could meet with each other and with men who were influential in public life, they could discuss their common frustrations, problems and difficulties, they could make plans to improve the status of women and further their own cause. The more they became aware of the evils and injustices in society, the more dissatisfied they were with the powerlessness of their sex and the National Association soon established itself as a pioneering organisation where emerging feminists were allowed a public voice.

One of the most influential women in the National Association was Barbara Bodichon[12], a cousin of Florence Nightingale and the daughter of Benjamin Smith, the radical Member of Parliament for Norwich. In a wealthy but highly enlightened family environment Barbara was encouraged in her political and literary interests. It was part of her father's philosophy that girls should receive an education equal to boys and so she was unusually well educated and he also provided her with a private income of £300 a year which guaranteed her independence. She married in 1857 at the age of thirty and eight years later, in 1865, she read the first ever paper on the subject of votes for women and subsequently became one of the key figures in the European suffrage struggle.

Each year the National Association for the Promotion of Social Science took its annual congress to the provinces and in October 1866 it so happened that Manchester was the chosen venue, an occasion which Lydia Becker could not miss with its rare opportunity to listen to a number of distinguished national figures. Barbara Bodichon was one of the speakers and, with her usual enthusiasm, she seized the opportunity to read again her paper *Reasons for the enfranchisement of women*.[13] In her lecture she reasoned that, under a representative government, any class which is not represented is likely to be neglected. There was a considerable number of women householders in the country who were expected to pay their rates and taxes yet were denied the privilege of their male counterparts to vote for their representative in Parliament. She argued in her address that

. . . among all the reasons for giving women votes, the one which appears to me the strongest, is that of the influence it might be expected to have in increasing public spirit . . . Give some women votes and it will tend to make all women think seriously of the concerns of the nation at large, and their interest having once been fairly roused, they will take pains, by reading and by consultation with persons better informed than themselves, to form sound opinions. As it is, women of the middle class occupy themselves but little with anything beyond their own family circle. They do not consider it any concern of theirs, if poor men and women are ill-nursed in workhouse infirmaries, and poor children ill-taught in workhouse schools. If the roads are bad, the drains neglected, the water poisoned, they think it is all very wrong, but it does not occur to them that it is their duty to get it put right. These farmer-women and business-women have honest sensible minds and much practical experience, but they do not bring their good sense to bear upon public affairs, because they think it is men's business, not theirs, to look after such things. It is this belief – so narrowing and deadening in its influence – that the exercise of the franchise would tend to dissipate. The mere fact of being called upon to enforce an opinion by a vote, would have an immediate effect in awakening a healthy sense of responsibility. There is no reason why these women should not take an active interest in all the social questions – education, public health, prison discipline, the poor laws and the rest – which occupy Parliament, and they would be much more likely to do so, if they felt they had importance in the eyes of Members of Parliament, and could claim a hearing for their opinions.

She pointed out that the most distinguished women in the country were disenfranchised, among them Florence Nightingale, Harriet Martineau and Louisa Twining,[14] and she concluded that the exclusion of female freeholders and householders from the franchise was an anomaly which any future Reform Bill should seek to remove.

Although Barbara Bodichon's paper was not considered of sufficient weight to be included in the reported transactions of the Association it certainly made a tremendous impact upon a solitary, quiet, thoughtful woman sitting in that large audience. Lydia Becker had gone along to the meeting totally ignorant of the developing suffrage movement but probably a little curious to find out what it was all about. Until that day she had been immersed in her own scientific interests and the demands of her family and had never given political work a thought. But Barbara Bodichon's impassioned plea for the enfranchisement of women was the blinding light on her personal road to Damascus, she emerged from that meeting having discovered her mission in life and from that day on until her death she devoted herself wholeheartedly to The Cause.

Chapter 3

WHILE listening to Barbara Bodichon at the National Association's congress Lydia Becker knew at once that she could and should be making a practical contribution to the struggle for women's suffrage; she considered her own talents and acknowledged to herself that she was a born organiser, she was conscientious and thorough in all that she did and she had a flair for clear, concise and persuasive writing which might be put to good effect.

In her address Barbara Bodichon had spoken about the first ever petition for the enfranchisement of women which had been presented to Parliament four months earlier. It had been made possible by the election to Parliament of John Stuart Mill[15] in the General Election of 1865. A staunch supporter of women's rights, he had taken the unprecedented step of including this hitherto taboo subject of women's suffrage at his first public meeting in St James's Hall and again in his election address. With another Reform Bill before Parliament which aimed to extend the franchise to all householders it seemed to Barbara Bodichon and her friends a propitious time to press women's claim for inclusion in the ranks of eligible voters, particularly as they now had such a sympathetic and articulate champion in the House of Commons. A working committee was set up to promote a parliamentary petition and John Stuart Mill promised to present it provided the organisers could guarantee him a hundred signatures. To the committee's own great astonishment 1499 signatures were collected without difficulty in little over a fortnight, and the signatories included such distinguished names as Florence Nightingale, Harriet Martineau, Josephine Butler and Mary Somerville.[16] In June 1866 two members of the committee, Emily Davies and Elizabeth Garrett,[17] undertook to deliver the petition to the House of Commons, but they were so embarrassed by the size of it and they felt so conspicuous standing with it in the lobby at Westminster that they almost took fright and persuaded an old apple woman who had a stall near the entrance to conceal it beneath her table until Mr Mill could be found. When he eventually arrived to meet the small deputation he was highly amused to find the petition thus hidden away, but was delighted at the large number of names it contained and exclaimed with great pleasure, 'Ah! this I can brandish with effect!'.

It was Lydia's constant regret that her name had not appeared on that original petition – if only she had been aware of the issue a few months sooner! – and she frequently used to say that there should have been a round 1500 signatures; hers should have been there. She lost no time, however, in offering her services to the London committee which, by now, had been properly constituted along more formal and permanent lines with the assistance of the Dean of Canterbury (Henry Alford)[18], and she was soon corresponding with Emily Davies who provided her with the text of a further petition which was to be signed by women householders setting out full particulars of the qualifications which should entitle women to vote. By January 1867 Lydia had sent a number of completed petition forms back to London and she wrote requesting a further supply. In her reply Emily Davies wrote with the news that a suffrage committee was to be set up in Manchester and she suggested that Lydia should in future work with them. It was surprising that Lydia did not already know about the preliminary meeting which had been held in Manchester on 11th January 1867 at the home of Dr Louis Borchardt when one of Manchester's parliamentary candidates, the radical Jacob Bright,[19] took the chair. Only six people were present at that meeting but it was nevertheless resolved to form a committee to promote the enfranchisement of women and to meet again in one month's time. It was at this second meeting, when twice the original number was present, that Lydia Becker was among them. She had already been active in her own way and came to the group bursting with enthusiasm and commitment, making her the obvious choice for secretary to the committee. She had found her role in life at the age of forty and an era of energetic activity had begun.

Even before she became involved with the Manchester committee Lydia had drafted an

Plate 3. A cartoon of Lydia Becker and Jacob Bright

article on female suffrage which she sent to Emily Davies in London for her comments. Emily read the paper with much interest and sent back a note of encouragement; it was her opinion that, although many of the arguments had been used before, there was a freshness in Lydia's manner of putting them which she believed merited its publication. She approached her friend Dean Alford who served with her on the London committee to suggest that the article should be published in the *Contemporary Review* of which he was the editor. It appeared in the issue for March 1867 and elicited much comment. Emily told Lydia that it had been much read and talked about and people were asking 'Who is this Miss Becker?'.

The article was simply called *Female Suffrage*, it ran to ten pages in the *Contemporary Review* and was subsequently reprinted as a pamphlet and widely distributed. In it Lydia referred to John Stuart Mill's historic speech in the House of Commons, probably the first occasion on which the claims of women to political rights had been seriously brought before Parliament, and she argued that, in an enquiring age, the principle of confining political privilege to men must be challenged:

It surely will not be denied that women have, and ought to have opinions of their own on subjects of public interest, and on the events which arise as the world wends on its way. But if it be granted that women may, without offence, hold political opinions, on what ground can the right be withheld of giving the same expression or effect to their opinions as that enjoyed by their male neighbours? . . . But to individual women the law says 'It is true that you are persons with opinions, wants, and wishes of your own, which you know better than any others can know for you; we allow that your stake and interest in the country are equal to that of your next-door-neighbour, and that your intelligence is not inferior to that of great numbers of male voters; we will tax your property and earnings as we see fit, but in return for your personal

TAXATION

AND

REPRESENTATION

Women Householders Pay the Town Rates and Vote in the Election of Town Councillors! That is fair!

Women Householders Pay the Queen's Taxes, but they are NOT allowed to Vote in the Election of the Members who Vote the Taxes! Is that fair?

Sign the Petition for Giving the FRANCHISE to WOMEN HOUSE-HOLDERS and RATE-PAYERS!

Plate 4.

Manchester Central Library

contribution to the national revenue you shall not possess the minutest fraction of political power; we will not allow you to have the smallest share in the government of the country of which you are a denizen, nor any voice in the making of the laws which determine the legal and political status of persons of your sex' . . .

It has been objected that conferring the franchise on women, and thus holding out to them an inducement to occupy their attention with political affairs, would tend to withdraw their minds from domestic duties . . . this

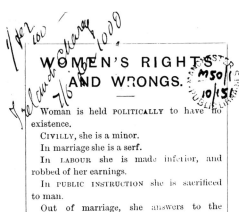

Plate 5.

Manchester Central Library

seems to imply that women are the only persons who have peculiar duties, and that the privilege of voting properly belongs to those who have nothing else to do . . . But experience proves that male voters are not, as a rule, in the habit of neglecting their private business in pursuit of political objects; why then should it be imagined that women, whose affections and interests lie yet more closely within the home circle, would be likely to neglect the duties naturally dear to them, for the sake of public affairs? . . .

'Women have nothing to do with politics' is a mere assertion, founded on sentimental, not on scientific grounds. It may be true, it may be false; it is a proposition fairly open to dispute. But though this proposition may be doubted, there is no doubt at all about its converse. It may be denied that women have anything to do with politics; it cannot be denied that politics have a great deal to do with women.[20]

Less than six months after she had confronted the issue of votes for women for the very first time, Lydia Becker had made her name in a nationally read periodical with a powerfully reasoned article which challenged the conventional assumptions of the day. The suffrage movement rejoiced that it had found another energetic and articulate champion, particularly since her efforts would extend the movement outside London and build up a strong following in the north of England.

In Manchester the new committee lost no time in allying itself with the London committee to promote the text of yet another petition, issued in London three months previously, and they issued a circular which stated that it was proposed during the current parliamentary session to present two petitions, one to be signed exclusively by women who were legally qualified to vote in all respects save that of sex, and the other by persons of all classes, both men and women. Emily Davies in London acted as Lydia's mentor and guide in those early days and a constant stream of letters passed between them,[21] with Emily advising Lydia step by step in the most effective way of collecting signatures and meeting the deadlines set for the submission of petitions. The two petitions were presented to the House of Commons in May 1867; one was signed by 1605 women householders and the other, from the general public, contained 3000 signatures. These strengthened John Stuart Mill's hand when he rose in the House on 20th May to move his amendment to the Representation of the People Bill:[22]

. . . to leave out the word 'man' in order to insert the word 'person' instead thereof.

Mill must have been on his feet at least forty-five minutes and he spoke with great eloquence and force:

Sir, within the limits of our Constitution this is a solitary case. There is no other example of an exclusion which is absolute. If the law denied a vote to all but the possessors of £5,000 a year, the poorest man in the nation might – and now and then would – acquire the suffrage; but

16

neither birth, nor fortune, nor merit, nor exertion, nor intellect, nor even that great disposer of human affairs, accident, can ever enable any woman to have her voice counted in those national affairs which touch her and hers as nearly as any other person in the nation.

. . . To lay a ground for refusing the suffrage to anyone, it is necessary to allege either personal unfitness or public danger. Now, can either of these be alleged in the present case? Can it be pretended that women who manage an estate or conduct a business – who pay rates and taxes, often to a large amount, and frequently from their own earnings – many of whom are responsible heads of families, and some of whom, in the capacity of school-mistresses, teach much more than a great number of the male electors have ever learnt – are not capable of a function of which every male householder is capable?

Mill returned to this argument concerning the personal fitness of women to exercise the vote later in his speech when he argued that enfranchisement would 'remove an unworthy stigma from the whole sex':

The law would cease to declare them incapable of serious things . . . They would no longer be classed with children, idiots and lunatics, as incapable of taking care of either themselves or others, and needing that everything should be done for them, without asking their consent.

He stressed that the 'silent domestic revolution' which had taken place could no longer be ignored, rigid demarcation lines between the roles of the sexes were no longer valid, men and women had become each other's companions:

. . . if women are frivolous, men will be frivolous; if women care for nothing but personal interest and idle vanities, men in general will care for little else; the two sexes must now either rise or sink together.

The second strand of his argument concerned the slogan 'No taxation without representation'

which had been coined by the Chartists some thirty years before and which was to be taken up by all sections of the suffrage movement into the twentieth century. Mill declared that to exclude women

. . . violates one of the oldest of our constitutional maxims – a doctrine dear to Reformers, and theoretically acknowledged by most Conservatives – that taxation and representation should be co-extensive.

and he concluded that

. . . if only one woman in 20,000 used the suffrage, to be declared capable of it would be a boon to all women.

The ensuing debate on Mill's amendment was of great interest, being the first of many in the House of Commons on the subject of women's suffrage. Opposition comments were revealing in their facetiousness. Viscount Galway urged Mill to withdraw his motion so that the House could proceed to more important business and advised him to 'stick to the Ballot, and leave the women alone'. Mr Laing thanked him for 'the pleasant interlude he had interposed to the grave and somewhat sombre discussions on the subject of Reform' and launched into a wild flight of fancy, asking the House to try and imagine such charming creatures as Juliet, Ophelia and Desdemona interesting themselves in and voting at elections. 'Which was most likely to figure in the character of a ratepayer or elector' he asked, 'the gentle Cordelia or the hateful and unattractive Goneril or Regan?'

The literal change in wording which Mill's amendment proposed was so minor as to appear merely a question of semantics today, but for the mid-Victorians it was a concept so far-reaching and revolutionary that, although he was listened to with considerable interest and curiosity, the House was not ready to accept such a radical change and his amendment was defeated by a majority of 123.

The opposition, on this and subsequent occasions, came from both sides of the House. Although there was considerable back-bench support on the Liberal side, Gladstone himself was opposed to female suffrage as a matter of self-interest, because he believed that women were more likely to vote Tory and, when it came to a division, many Liberals voted against the measure rather than incur the displeasure of their leader and possibly prejudice their own parliamentary careers. Disraeli, on the other hand, professed a certain sympathy for the women's cause, but the majority of Tory members thought otherwise. Some, like Mr Beresford-Hope[23] in a later debate, expressed high-minded sentiments about the very nature of women calling for the most chivalrous and protective treatment on the part of men, but it is more likely that he and his fellow Tories on the back benches saw the issue as a serious threat to their male-dominated world and something to be vigorously resisted. In an Establishment fiercely loyal to the Crown, Victoria's known antipathy to women's rights was an influential factor and those who campaigned against women's suffrage found it convenient to ignore the glaring anomaly of a constitution which allowed a woman to hold the highest office of state while denying her female subjects any participation.

The infant suffrage societies were not despondent at the outcome. The Cause had been firmly placed on the political agenda and 73 Members of Parliament had shown their support. This was the foundation upon which they could build and thoughts turned to ways of strengthening their organisation.

Having devoted so much time to organising petitions Lydia realised that she now needed the backing of a properly constituted suffrage society in Manchester with an actively participating membership. In June 1867 she drew up a draft constitution for 'The Society for the Promotion of the Enfranchisement of Women' which she circulated to all members of the committee. The object of the society would be 'to obtain for women the right of voting for Members of Parliament on the same conditions as it is, or may be, granted to men' and the suggested annual subscription was not less than one shilling. The constitution was finalised in August, Lydia's rather unwieldy name was abandoned in favour of a title in line with London, and so the Manchester National Society for Women's Suffrage came into being. Lydia had been working closely with the London Society and had benefited from its support and advice and she was very aware that much would be gained by mutual co-operation and learning from each other. At much the same time similar suffrage societies had sprung up in Edinburgh, Birmingham and Bristol and she believed that it would be to their great mutual advantage, besides lending strength and weight to their cause, if they formed themselves into some sort of federal union. Accordingly the Manchester Society passed a resolution in November 1867:

> That this Society agrees that its members shall unite with members of the Societies having the same object, to form one National Society for Women's Suffrage with independent centres of action; the constitution, executive and funds of each Society shall remain entirely irresponsible to and uncontrolled by the others, the bond of union to consist solely in the assumption of the name National Society for Women's Suffrage, and the amalgamation of the names of members enrolled by each centre into one national list of supporters of the political enfranchisement of women.[24]

It would clearly be advantageous to have a national membership so that the strength of support throughout the whole country could be fairly assessed. Similar resolutions were soon adopted by the other societies and so, due in large measure to Lydia's bold initiative, the large and influential National Society for Women's Suffrage (NSWS) came into being.

The aims of the movement were modest; there was no question at that time of universal suffrage, even for men, and the women's suffrage societies were campaigning only for the extension of the franchise to women on the same terms as already existed for men. With the Married Women's Property Act of 1882 still fourteen years away, only a very limited number of women, mainly spinsters and widows, would have possessed the requisite property qualifications. In 1868 a wife's property still passed automatically to her husband upon marriage, except in the few instances where property had been settled specifically upon the woman for her separate use independently of her husband, so almost all married women, together with most poorer women, who had no property qualification anyway, were excluded from the vote. Today the demands of the early suffragists seem modest enough, but in the mid-nineteenth century they were revolutionary. However, the issue of excluding married women was one which was later to divide the movement and cause much unhappiness and recrimination.

But, in 1868, Lydia's early success in consolidating support for The Cause nationwide and the great surge of interest generated by the Reform Act of 1867 led her to believe that the battle was more than half won and achievement of their goals within sight. In a mood of optimism and euphoria she wrote to a friend:

> I must make a vigorous effort to beg for money in Manchester, to go on. I do believe that if we are thoroughly bent on our point, and play our cards well, we may see women voting at the next election, and I am quite sure that if they do not vote then it will be the last general election from which they will be excluded.[25]

Time was to prove her very wrong.

Chapter 4

WHILE the suffragists had found in John Stuart Mill a parliamentary champion who was prepared to plead their case on the floor of the House of Commons, there were other supporters who, with equal enthusiasm, had been researching the validity of women's suffrage in law. The young solicitor Dr Richard Pankhurst[26] who served with Lydia Becker on the executive committee of the Manchester Society co-operated with a sympathetic barrister, Thomas Chisholm Anstey,[27] and between them they uncovered a large mass of curious evidence, hitherto buried in old documents and reports, which showed that women had once had ancient legal rights to the vote. Anstey published their findings in a paper which set out to prove that there was no constitutional impediment to the enfranchisement of women. He claimed that in feudal times the right of appointing parliamentary representatives had depended upon property and not upon sex and he unearthed fascinating records in support of his argument which proved that female landowners and freewomen of certain towns had in the past exercised their right to vote. In particular he cited the case of Anne Clifford, Countess of Dorset, who not only claimed and exercised all the ancient rights which went with her title but went further and, despite the protestations of the Secretary of State, nominated her own grandson to be a Member of Parliament in 1667.

With the publication of Anstey's researches the idea that to admit women to the vote was an unheard of innovation began to give way to the view that women were already entitled to all the benefits of the Representation of the People Act of 1867 and that neither a statute nor a judicial decision could be found which declared them ineligible to vote. These discoveries gave great encouragement to the members of the newly established Manchester Society and at the suggestion of Dr Richard Pankhurst and with his valuable guidance they resolved to concentrate their efforts on this particular issue, to take advantage of the confused state of the law and to campaign to have women ratepayers placed upon the electoral register. An anomaly in the 1867 Act which had established household suffrage gave further weight to their case. The great Reform Act of 1832 had referred throughout specifically to *male persons*, but in the drafting of the new Act of 1867 the word *man* had been substituted. John Stuart Mill had sought, in his amendment, to replace the word *man* by the less specific word *person*, but this had been defeated. Yet, strangely enough, another amendment to substitute *male person* was also defeated and the bill passed into law with the word *man* used throughout. Dr Pankhurst's legal mind argued that the use of the generic term *man* implied that all householders were now enfranchised, both men and women, and he urged the Manchester Society to put the question to the test by challenging the Boards of Overseers who were responsible for compiling the electoral registers. Lydia agreed with him wholeheartedly; to her logical mind the term *man* was usually understood to refer to both sexes and she supported her argument with the biblical quotation 'God made man in his own image; male and female created he them'. Furthermore, she gave wide publicity to Lord Brougham's Interpretation Act of 1850,[28] an act 'to shorten the language of Acts of Parliament', which had stipulated that 'in all acts words importing the masculine gender shall be deemed and taken to include females . . . unless the contrary to gender is expressly provided'. There was no such provision in the Representation of the People Act of 1867 and the ratepaying clauses of that act, in which masculine pronouns were used throughout, were also applied to women. It was not difficult for Lydia to argue with considerable justification that if, in one and the same Act of Parliament, the ratepaying clauses applied to both men and women ratepayers, then the voting clauses must also apply to both sexes. Furthermore, it was not only unjust but unlawful to include women in the clauses which imposed the burden of paying rates but to exclude them from the clauses which conferred the privilege of exercising a vote. She was nevertheless realistic enough to know that this argument would not in itself be sufficient to persuade local overseers of the registry that the women had a valid case and it was clear that, in Manchester alone, some seven thousand women would still be excluded from the electoral register. She believed that the only remedy was to mount a full scale campaign to persuade all the excluded women to submit a formal claim to the overseers to be placed on the registers and the overseers, in turn, would be bound to present all such claims to a revising barrister for adjudication. The campaign was not restricted to Manchester; although the initial impetus had come from Dr Pankhurst, Lydia made contact with the London, Bristol and Birmingham suffrage societies and persuaded them to co-operate with her in this project. At that time the suffrage societies were still in their infancy and this was to be the first real test of their strength. They may have been naive in supposing that such radical change could be brought about as the result of a single campaign, but there is no doubt that they were fired with enthusiasm and in a high state of excitement; they felt that they had justice on their side, that their right to vote had been unquestionably established and all that remained was to reclaim that ancient right.

It was in this mood of euphoria that an incident occurred in Manchester towards the end of 1867 which brought further hope and encouragement. By some accident a woman's name had slipped on to the electoral register. A day or two before a by-election was due to take place someone noticed the name of Mrs Lily Maxwell

on the list of parliamentary voters and drew it to the attention of Lydia Becker who lost no time in hurrying round to Lily Maxwell's house to persuade her to use her vote. Fortunately Mrs Maxwell did not need much persuasion, she was just the sort of person the suffragists would have selected for a test case, and she entered into the spirit of the challenge with enthusiasm. She was a widow who supported herself by running a small crockery shop, and she was a woman of decided and positive political convictions. She announced herself a warm admirer of the Liberal candidate, Jacob Bright who was a great supporter of women's suffrage, and she was only too happy to be able to cast a vote for him, declaring that if she had had twenty votes she would have given them all to Jacob Bright.

On the great day, 26th November 1867, Lydia Becker and another member of her committee accompanied Lily Maxwell to Jacob Bright's committee rooms and from there a number of Bright's male supporters escorted the ladies to the polling station. At that time there was no voting by ballot and votes were cast publicly, the occasion having something of a revivalist meeting, with cheers and jeers from a motley crowd assembled in the booth as each vote was cast. It was therefore felt to be improper that women should even enter the polling station, but as Mrs Maxwell's name appeared on the list of electors the returning officer had no choice but to accept her vote. When she had made her historic vote all the men in the room, both Jacob Bright's supporters and his opponents, gave three hearty cheers for the heroine of the occasion. There had been none of the anticipated rowdyism or opposition and someone present, perhaps Lydia herself, was reported as saying that there had been less inconvenience from the crowd than is often experienced at a public concert or fashionable chapel.

Lydia took the success of this small adventure as a good omen and she wrote immediately to the secretary of the Manchester overseers to plead the case for the inclusion of women ratepayers on the register. He replied that he did not intend placing women's names on the register because he was not satisfied of their eligibility to vote and by including them wrongly on the register he laid himself open to a penalty of fifty pounds, whereas there was no penalty for wrongful omission from the register. This only confirmed what Lydia already knew but it was the official signal to launch her ambitious campaign and this she did by organising a large public meeting in the assembly room of the Free Trade Hall in Manchester on 14th April 1868.

This meeting was later regarded as a major landmark in the history of the movement. Not only was it the first truly public meeting to be held on the question of women's suffrage, it was also the first in this country to be addressed by women, although a few had given lectures or read papers at specialised gatherings, and it formulated the policy which was to be pursued from then on by all the women's suffrage societies acting in unison. The organisation of that meeting was the first major test for the Manchester Society and no one could predict the likely response. Even Lydia admitted to being unnerved by the occasion but she was ably supported and encouraged by her friend Mr Pochin,[29] the mayor of Salford, who agreed to take the chair. The first resolution to be passed that evening was moved by Lydia herself and it made explicit the aims of the women's suffrage movement in the following words:

> . . . that the exclusion of women from the exercise of the franchise in the election of Members of Parliament being unjust in principle and inexpedient in practice, this meeting is of the opinion that the right of voting should be granted to them on the same terms as it is or may be granted to men.

This was seconded by Archdeacon Sandford and supported by Mr F.B. Potter MP and Dr Richard Pankhurst. The second resolution was moved by the mayor's wife, Mrs Pochin;[29]

> . . . that this meeting expresses its cordial approval of the objects of the National Society for Women's Suffrage, and of the course it has

Plate 6. Lydia Becker in 1874, a portrait from *The Graphic*.

Mary Evans Picture Library

hitherto pursued, and pledges itself to support its future efforts by all practical and constitutional methods, especially by urging women possessing legal qualifications to claim to be put on the Parliamentary register.

This was seconded by the lawyer Thomas Chisholm Anstey and supported by the recently elected Member of Parliament, Jacob Bright. The resolutions had been drawn up by a local lawyer, the Manchester coroner at the time, and made quite clear the campaigners' intention to work constitutionally, within the framework of the law. There was never any hint or suggestion of civil disobedience which would have been unthinkable to Lydia and her colleagues. The success of the Manchester meeting prompted the Birmingham Society to follow suit and on 18th April Lydia wrote to Mary Johnson, secretary of the Birmingham Society, urging her to go ahead:

> I am delighted to hear how well you are progressing in Birmingham and that you

contemplate a public meeting. Our success ought to be at once an encouragement and an incentive to such a step. Our resolution will then have been moved by Manchester, seconded by Birmingham, and must be accepted by the country.

Mary Johnson's reply to this letter must have struck a chord of friendship because in May Lydia sent her a small trinket as a thank-you for running the committee and, besides the practical business of advising her that the Birmingham Society should take care not to become identified with any one political party, she allowed herself a rare personal revelation:

> I feel much flattered by the way you write to me. I have never had an elder sister or brother, or anyone near me to lean on . . . sympathy is what one longs for.[30]

These comments were made at a time when her health was beginning to give way under the strain of so much concentrated activity. In early April she had written to Jessie Boucherett expressing her frustration at being 'a prisoner in my own home', unable to walk but unable to afford a carriage, and requesting the use of some mission funds for the purpose. She was depressed because there was so much to be done and she felt that she was failing the movement at a critical time through her enforced physical inactivity. The letter was struck through and possibly never sent and, later the same month when she had occasion to write a long business letter to Jessie she merely allowed herself the incidental comment:

> I feel almost overwhelmed with work, and my strength wretchedly feeble. If I were strong or rich, I could do so much!

Her main preoccupation in the spring of 1868 was the campaign aimed at persuading women householders to submit claims for inclusion on the electoral register. Although the time for making such claims was not until the first three weeks in August, Lydia was well aware that she would need all of three or four months to organise her campaign. She believed in planning down to the finest detail and was never one to leave things until the last minute. She said herself that she did not want to be still organizing her army when she should be marching them off to the field. Although she had set herself the target of finding two thousand women who would be prepared to submit claims, which she felt would be an impressive enough number, her plan involved visiting every one of the seven thousand women householders in Manchester, explaining to each of them the state of the law, finding out which of them would be willing to submit a claim when the time came, making careful notes of their names and addresses so that they only had to take them the application form at the appropriate time, get them filled in, signed and delivered in bulk to the overseers of the registry. It is not known how many active workers she gathered round her for the house-to-house visitation but it must have been a formidable undertaking in an age when you did not simply pick up a telephone and most probably had no transport of your own.

She relied on the personal approach to explain and persuade women to join in the campaign and must have been overjoyed at the response which was way above the target she had set herself. However, the very fact that over five thousand women agreed to request registration meant that each of them had to be visited a second time to be given the appropriate forms and to ensure that they were properly completed and signed. The women's claims came before local overseers of the register in the first instance and a few of these overseers took it upon themselves to dismiss them, but the great majority were passed on to revising barristers who found themselves inundated with applications from shoals of women claiming what they believed to be their constitutional rights. One of the revising barristers was the women's champion, Thomas Chisholm Anstey, and of course the claims which came before him and some other like minded members of the bar were allowed to stand, but in the majority of cases the women were turned down and then had the right of appeal to the High Court.

Throughout September 1868 the women's applications were being heard before revising barristers in and around Manchester and Lydia was kept busy travelling all over the area to lend her personal support. It was an exhausting time for her as on the occasion when she had to leave Manchester at six thirty in the morning to travel the thirty of so miles to Ormskirk in time for a hearing, but she was delighted with the outcome which fully justified the effort and she was able to write to Jessie Boucherett the following day 'We came off with flying colours in Ormskirk yesterday'. Perhaps it was prophetic that the first eleven women to be heard there had come from the small township of Lydiate where there was some doubt as to the validity of the notices objecting to the women. The revising barrister took exception to the notices and ruled that all the votes objected to, whether men or women, should remain on the register. The same thing happened when thirty women from Scarisbrick came up for consideration. However, in one instance it was decided to overrule the technical disqualification and to take the case on its merits, as a kind of test case, and Margaret Ackers was called upon to prove her qualification. She was duly questioned as to her status and occupation and the amount of rates she paid, and then the revising barrister, Mr Foald, pronounced her vote a good one under the terms of the Representation of the People Act of 1867. The Tory agent who was present immediately objected to the decision and asked for an appeal, which was granted. However, Lydia was delighted to discover another revising barrister besides her ally Thomas Chisholm Anstey who was prepared to give a judicial decision that the new act extended the franchise to women.

Successful hearings such as those at Ormskirk created a wave of optimism in the Society, yet there was always the lurking fear that perhaps it would not be so easy to break down years of prejudice and Lydia was realistic enough to know that the traditional conservatism of the judiciary might well cause the High Court decision to go against them when the appeals

were heard. At one moment she could write in optimistic mood 'I have been, and am still busily engaged in looking up the legal arguments, in conjunction with our counsel, and it seems to me impossible to find a flaw in them', but at other times she declared that she had no faith in the impartiality of the tribunal, although she dared to hope that perhaps one judge might rule in the women's favour.

It was in this mood of hopeful expectancy and less optimistic realism that the Manchester Society met for its first annual general meeting on 30th October 1868. The committee agreed to book Manchester Town Hall for the meeting. It was a major decision at the time and represented a great act of faith. Indeed, Lydia wrote to one of the speakers a few days beforehand 'I tremble, for it is a bold venture to come out into the Town Hall, and I fear lest we should not get fifty people there'. She need not have worried. When the day came people thronged to the meeting, the hall was packed to the doors and the occasion even attracted a reporter from *The Times*. Jacob Bright told Lydia that he had come hardly expecting to find a dozen or twenty people and was astonished to see the room full. The report in *The Times* on 3rd November concentrated on 'the glorious uncertainty of the law' which allowed individual revising barristers to come to widely differing decisions concerning women's right to vote for Members of Parliament. Referring to the imminent appeals in the High Court the writer concluded that:

… if one supposes it was ever the intention of legislature to give women a vote, and if they do get it, it will be by a sort of accident, in itself objectionable, though in its practical consequences perhaps harmless enough. On the other hand, if they are refused it, the nation will, no doubt, be formally and in the light of day committing itself, through its judicial tribunal, to the dangerous doctrine that representation need not go along with taxation.

The case of the 5346 women householders of Manchester came before the High Court in the Court of Common Pleas early in November

1868 in the presence of Lord Chief Justice Bovill and Justices Willes, Keating and Byles and the case became known technically as *Chorlton v. Lings*. It was one of four test cases which were to be heard and Lydia travelled to London for the hearing. Sir John Coleridge QC[31] appeared as counsel for the women with Richard Pankhurst as his junior. Pankhurst had undertaken an immense amount of research in preparation for the case which was presented with great judicial scholarship. Sir John spoke eloquently of the ancient constitutional right of women to take part in parliamentary elections and he produced a number of documents from the Record Office to support his arguments, including indentures returning Members of Parliament which bore the signatures of women. He also argued that the general term *man* used in the new Representation of the People Act must be taken to include women, not only generally but also specifically. However, all the well-researched arguments were of no avail and the bench was unanimous in its decision against the women. In rather pompous comments Mr Justice Byles trusted that their unanimous decision would for ever exorcise and lay the ghost of a doubt which ought never to have made its appearance, and Mr Justice Willles went further, pointing out that their decision was not based upon any underrating of the female sex but that exemption from voting was founded upon motives of decorum and was a privilege of the female sex.

Lydia had sat intently in the gallery throughout the proceedings. If she was discouraged by the final judgement she did not allow her disappointment to deflect her from the next step in her thoroughly planned campaign. In anticipation of an adverse result the women of her committee in Manchester had painstakingly produced by hand eight hundred letters addressed to every single candidate in the general election which was due to take place the following week. As soon as judgement was given Lydia slipped out of the court and telegraphed to Manchester the cryptic message 'post your letters'. And so, the very next day, with the case still uppermost in everyone's minds and reported in the press, each parliamentary candidate received the following communication:

> Sir, – The decision in the Court of Common Pleas having been adverse to the claims of women to vote in the election of Members of Parliament, a Bill will be introduced into the House of Commons to establish their right to vote on the same conditions as men.
>
> Will you kindly inform me whether you will, if returned, support such a Bill?
>
> I am, Sir, your obedient servant,
>
> Lydia E. Becker.

Her aim was to ensure that the first note of agitation throughout the country should coincide with the public announcement of the High Court decision.

Chapter 5

IN the week before the appeals were heard in the High Court, Lydia had declared to a friend that she would regard an adverse decision with a sense of deepest humiliation, yet in her heart of hearts she knew what the result would be and when judgement was given she was not particularly dispirited but threw herself with typical vigour into the next phase of the campaign.

With a general election imminent she was determined to assert the validity of the women's claims. Some women's names had already been placed, or allowed to stay, on the electoral register by a few sympathetic revising barristers and those women were not affected by the High Court decision. It was vital that this tiny minority of women with a valid vote should make an impact on election day. In Manchester there were thirteen of them and Lydia approached each one of them personally, pointing out to them that they were privileged in having the right to vote and exhorting them to use it. On polling day eight of the thirteen plucked up sufficient courage to vote, a gentleman generously put his carriage and pair of greys at Lydia's disposal and, in unaccustomed style, she accompanied each of the women in turn to the polling station. She described to Jessie Boucherett how she had spent all day ferrying her eight women voters from their homes and back again and how madly jealous the Tories had been when they found out that all these women had voted Liberal. When the Tory agent protested, Lydia replied that she did know of one woman who would vote Tory if he would care to go and fetch her himself. He jumped at the opportunity, even taking his candidate's own carriage to fetch her. This was exactly what Lydia had hoped for; as she said, it committed the Tory party to the principle of women's suffrage and so they could make no political objection to the Liberals'

support of The Cause. She wrote to Jessie the same night:

> It was better that they should fetch her spontaneously than that I should bring her, and it would have gone terribly against the grain to have taken a woman to vote, not only against my own side in politics, but for a candidate (Mr Birley) opposed to women's right.

It seems that in neighbouring Salford the few women left on the register were eagerly competed for by the opposing candidates. Lydia also managed to be in Salford that day, drumming up support, and telling each of the women that they must vote for their own man and not be influenced by her personal political views. It seems that ten women voted, four for one party and six for the other, and one wonders what determined their choice. Those who gave their vote to a candidate who professed no sympathy for the women's cause were more likely to have been influenced by traditional voting patterns in their own families rather than by any burning desire to increase support for women's suffrage in the House of Commons. For Lydia it had been an exhausting day but the excitement of it all was not conducive to sleep and, having no one to talk it over with, she wrote to her various friends until late into the night to recount the day's events, closing with the words 'I ought to go to bed, or I shall be used up in the morning'.

When the results of the general election became known the suffragists were encouraged to discover that some ninety members favourable to The Cause had been returned to Parliament, an increase of twelve on the previous Parliament, but they had suffered one devastating blow, the defeat of their chief spokesman and champion John Stuart Mill in the Westminster constituency. *The Times* commented upon a very corrupt campaign by his Conservative opponent W. H. Smith, the newspaper distributor, who managed to turn Mill's previous majority of seven hundred in the 1865 election to a majority double that size for himself three years later. Women suffragists were shattered by the loss of their leading parliamentary spokesman and supporter and Lydia exclaimed in despair to a friend 'The defeat of Mr Mill is a crushing blow; how shall we fare in the House of Commons bereft of his giant strength'.

However, the abrupt and untimely end to Mill's parliamentary career at least enabled him to channel his energies into writing and he immediately resumed work on his most famous book *On the subjection of women* which was published the following year in 1869, enjoying a wide readership and promoting the suffragists' cause in a different and no less powerful way. The book had been gestating for many years; it had been inspired by his wife Harriet who had died eight years previously, and he had received considerable help and support from his stepdaughter Helen Taylor in preparing the final manuscript for the press.

With the loss of Mill's powerful presence in the House of Commons there was parliamentary deadlock on the issue of women's suffrage and, although there were sympathisers who tried by all possible means to secure debates on the subject they met with steady hostility and any opposing speeches, far from being temperate and well reasoned, were almost always sexist and facetious. One member, speaking in 1870, remarked that he 'did not like to see women enter into competition with dancing dogs, to show their wonderful powers in doing things which it is not expected they will do' and Earl Percy drew cheap laughs from the House by painting an amusing picture of a female Prime Minister too absorbed with her approaching confinement to attend to affairs of state.

The committee of the Manchester Society met after the 1868 election result to formulate its next strategy in the light of John Stuart Mill's defeat. Until now members had concentrated their efforts upon challenging the legality of the composition of the electoral registers but had been turned down by the great majority of revising barristers and, on appeal, by the High Court as well. They felt that the time had come to take their case directly to Parliament without further delay. Lydia, in particular, was searching for new constitutional means to further The Cause and there is no doubt that it was her clear-sightedness and resolve which directed the policy of the whole movement at this time. Her proposal was to seek the co-operation of sympathetic Members of Parliament in order to get a bill introduced at the first opportunity. In January 1869 the Manchester committee resolved to approach their own Member of Parliament, Jacob Bright, who was one of their active supporters, asking him to confer with Russell Gurney[32] and other sympathetic members in the House with a view to introducing a measure on women's suffrage in the forthcoming parliamentary session. Lydia was hoping for instant action but Bright and Gurney counselled a less impetuous approach. They knew only too well the importance of preparing the ground thoroughly before the introduction of such a measure, they knew that they must have public sympathy on their side and they advised that any bill should be deferred for a session to give the suffrage societies plenty of time to work upon public opinion by means of a well orchestrated programme of meetings and petitions. Lydia had already written to her friend Miss Taunton 'I earnestly hope that we shall not need a *petition*', but if she was disappointed at the prospect of delay she concealed it well, urging her members to even greater and more serious efforts and acknowledging for the first time that they could not hope for immediate, perhaps not even speedy success and that ultimate victory would only be accomplished by a long course of systematic and persevering agitation.

But sustained campaigns need money and so fund raising became a major preoccupation. Recognising the importance of long term support Mrs Jacob Bright[33] undertook to find a few friends who would each guarantee a sum of one hundred pounds, to be given in five annual instalments of twenty pounds, and about this time too Lydia's good friend Mr Thomas Thomasson of Bolton became a regular and generous benefactor to the Manchester Society and his donations relieved the committee of a great deal of financial worry and uncertainty.

Local committees were being set up in many places in order to collect names on petitions and Lydia watched over them with all the maternal concern of a hen for her brood; she was anxious for their success but wise enough not to interfere, believing that 'like a newly married couple they will best settle to their work if left to themselves'. Sometimes she was disappointed with the failure of a new group as on the occasion when the secretary of the Birmingham Society wrote to her to report that their attempt to set up a group in Coventry had failed because 'the lady to whom I last applied wrote that she considered our zeal overforward'.

As a consequence of all this local activity Lydia suddenly found herself much in demand as a speaker, and she began travelling regularly all over the north of England, from Manchester to Leeds, Newcastle and many other towns. Being somewhat reticent by temperament she was not a natural speaker and she worried constantly about the kind of reception she might receive and whether her voice would carry in a large hall. Women speakers were such a novelty that they inevitably attracted a large crowd, many of whom turned up out of sheer curiosity rather than with any real interest in the topic of the meeting and they tended to judge the speaker more by her hairstyle and the cut of her dress rather than by what she had to say. For Lydia public speaking was always something of an ordeal. She was naturally of a rather serious demeanour and, when nervousness stifled her smile and banished her sense of humour, it was said that she appeared more like a valkyrie of the political arena than the sensitive, kindly person that she really was underneath. Chronic back pain gave her an unnaturally stiff posture, she tended to dress severely and wore her thick hair plaited and coiled on top of her head and narrow, steel rimmed spectacles. She was well aware that

she might face a barrage of gibes and sneers, but she allowed neither sarcasm nor heckling to deflect her from her purpose. She overcame prejudice by raising the issue of women's rights to the level of serious debate so that many who came to mock and have a cheap evening's entertainment at her expense went away converted to The Cause.

In the early days of the campaign it took considerable courage for her to stand up in front of an audience, but she never allowed her nervousness to show and, however much she trembled inwardly, she gained a reputation for speaking calmly and clearly in a strong, sweet voice and always going straight to the point.

Her first ever lecture tour began in Leeds where she was particularly well received and, on the motion of a Mr Hickes in the audience, her address was subsequently printed in a cheap form which allowed for wide distribution. Yet Lydia herself had been deeply troubled and apprehensive about her public appearance in Leeds and felt afterwards that she had not performed at all well. She was always her own sternest critic and, with a whole series of lectures before her, she confided her fears in a letter to her friend Miss Holland:

> I am bewildered, puzzled, unnerved and dissatisfied about my lecture, and unable to see my way clearly to mend matters, while the time is very short for any improvement. I believe I should do much better speaking than reading, but have not sufficient practice to make it safe to trust to mere notes for the pièce de résistance of the evening; my only chance is to trust to a discussion, to something being said that will give me the opportunity to reply. Learning a lecture by heart is quite out of the question. My peculiar nervous organization makes such a feat absolutely impossible.[34]

Although she never mastered the art of impromptu speaking, she became more confident and relaxed with the passage of time so that she could allow herself the occasional humorous remark which would draw forth encouraging laughter and applause from her audience as they warmed to her and she to them.

She felt very keenly the absence of a husband or close confidante with whom she could share her experiences – her moods of elation when a meeting had gone well, or her misgivings when she felt that she had done badly – and she turned more and more to sympathetic friends of The Cause for advice and support. For all her public activity she was at heart a lonely woman who unburdened herself in voluminous correspondence, frequently sitting down at the end of a very full day to write two or three long personal letters. It is not difficult to imagine her alone in a hotel room after an inspiring and exhausting meeting, the events of the evening churning over and over in her mind so that she was unable to sleep. With no one to share the experience with her she found her only outlet for her emotions in long, descriptive letters to friends. She once confessed to Ursula Bright:

> I get very weary sometimes . . . the worst time for me is when I wake early in the morning – I often feel quite wretched then, but fresher after I get up and then feel quite strong. When I am anxious or perplexed, or see obstacles in our path, all my physical strength seems to collapse, but it comes again when matters brighten up. It does me good to know that you approve of what we are doing.[35]

Her family were not enthusiastic about her suffrage activities and she had little support from them. Although she wrote regularly to her brothers she confined herself largely to family matters and once wrote to Leigh that she felt he would not be much interested in what she was doing, although she believed that she was helping to shape history. Her radical views were inherited from her grandfather, but she used to say that her grandmother was a red hot Tory – as was her own father, Hannibal – and she felt ostracised by her family on account of her liberalism and especially for her views on the emancipation of women. Her relationship with her father had always been strained and deteriorated further when he felt obliged to resign his membership of the exclusive Tory club in Manchester, John Shaw's, because he was reluctant to have to explain the feminist activities of his eldest daughter to the committee.

If Lydia had had her father's sympathy for the crusade she was embarked upon, it is possible that she might also have had financial support from him for her work. But she was always restricted for lack of money and, although she must have received some kind of personal allowance, it was nowhere near enough to enable her to continue without constant anxiety about funds. She received a small honorarium from the Manchester Society to cover her expenses, but sometimes a campaign was in danger of collapse because the money was exhausted and Lydia had no private means to fall back upon. In a letter to Mary Wolstenholme about the door to door canvass of women householders she wrote:

> My fund for the canvass is absolutely at an end and I am continuing it in faith this week. But we have two women at work who each get about 90 claims a day and I cannot find it in my heart to stop them till I have made another desperate effort.[36]

In the same letter she said that she was writing a paper that she was due to read at the British Association meeting in Norwich, that it was 'desperately hard work' but 'the one great test of the year for me'. Yet, at the same time, she was worrying about how she was going to pay for her board and lodging in Norwich. She was appalled at the high prices being charged – 7/6d a night – which far exceeded the amount she had saved and put aside to cover both her fare and her accommodation. Eventually she persuaded the editor of the *Manchester Examiner and Times* to engage her as his special correspondent in Norwich for the week of the meetings, and although this extra commitment imposed an added strain upon her at least the fees she earned helped pay her expenses.

Her sister Esther was the only member of the family to show any interest in Lydia's public life and even she did not allow herself to become too closely involved. She would sometimes assist by cutting out press notices and advertisements from the newspapers and sending them to Lydia's supporters, and she would also sell tickets for public meetings, but she seems to have drawn the line at actually accompanying her sister to her speaking engagements. Whether this was reluctance on her part to show open support for Lydia in the face of their father's disapproval, or whether she felt that she could serve a more useful purpose in maintaining a harmonious domestic routine at home, we shall never know. But it is certain that, as far as her family was concerned, Lydia ploughed a lonely furrow.

With family support conspicuously lacking Lydia turned more and more to the company of like-minded friends. She was always a welcome guest at the home of Jacob Bright, one of the city's Members of Parliament, who also served on the executive committee of the Manchester Society. He came from a well-known Lancashire family of Quakers and his more famous brother John had helped to found the Anti-Corn Law League with Richard Cobden. Because she knew that John Bright was not a convinced suffragist Lydia was at first prejudiced against his brother Jacob, but she soon realised that the two men were very different and she came under the spell of his gentleness and goodness and admired his evenly balanced mind. Jacob was not as strong as his brother either physically or intellectually and Lydia wrote that she feared the effects of fatigue on her 'dear and trusted friend' who suffered from a delicate chest and a tendency towards bronchitis. When Parliament was in recess Lydia spent many happy weekends with Jacob and his wife Ursula at their home in Alderley Edge and Jacob would take her back to town in his carriage on Monday mornings. During the parliamentary session the Brights lived in London and Lydia always looked forward to the time when they would return north and she could once again enjoy their delightful companionship and share their pleasure in their young family – she was especially fond of their first daughter whom she

described as 'a perfect beauty'.

Another member of the executive committee upon whom Lydia relied heavily was the young solicitor Dr Richard Pankhurst. He was a brilliant lawyer and an outstanding public personality who used all his talents in the cause of popular reform and, although he was considerably younger than Lydia she looked up to him and admired his original mind and was much influenced by his superior knowledge in all the legal aspects of electoral reform. In June 1868 she wrote to her brother, Leigh:

> I like Dr Pankhurst – he is a clever little man with plenty to say – and some strange ideas – it is refreshing to meet with people whose actions get out of the ordinary groove.[37]

When Richard's daughter Sylvia came to write her history of the suffragette movement in 1931 she attributed much of the early success of the Manchester Society to her father's influence and went so far as to say that Lydia's confident reliance upon him caused many of their acquaintances to anticipate a romance which never materialised. A considerable amount of correspondence passed between them with Lydia frequently asking him to supply her with facts and statistics which she could use as ammunition. In the campaign to have women householders included on the electoral registers Richard Pankhurst had argued powerfully with the overseers and the deputations which he led aroused great interest and discussion. Lydia was profoundly grateful for his help and expertise and wrote to him:

> My dear Dr Pankhurst, . . .
>
> I suppose our campaign among the Overseers is over, and I have had it on my mind to endeavour to express to you my sense of gratitude and obligation to you for consenting to act for us, and admiration of the great powers of reasoning and of oratory you have displayed. It has been a hard, uphill fight – against hopeless odds, but if any man could have won – you are he! . . .
>
> You must have bestowed great labours and

hard thoughts upon your speeches, and I beg you not to think that we are unconscious of the magnitude of the gift you have so freely and generously made us. It is no light thing that you have done and you must not think that we estimate lightly the cost at which you have done it . . .

    Yours truly

    Lydia E. Becker[38]

Apart from her colleagues on the executive committee Lydia's friends were mostly far flung; they did not often meet and the letters which passed between them became precious symbols of the support which existed outside her immediate circle in Manchester. Her friends were frequently addressed with greater intimacy than her immediate family and she felt able to express herself more freely to them. She sought to break down the conventional Victorian formality between correspondents, addressing her friend Mary Wolstenholme as 'My dear Mary' and confiding her antipathy for 'the odious "Miss" – let it be forever banished from between us'. Never one to suffer fools gladly, she was frequently frustrated by the follies of those whose co-operation she needed and she found an outlet for her annoyance in her letters to Mary to whom she could express an honest opinion of those who crossed her path without fear of giving offence:

The Mayor of Manchester has vindicated his reputation for being a stupid ass by refusing to sign the petition.

Another cherished correspondent was Josephine Butler whose letters, Lydia wrote, 'are pearls when they come'. She felt secure enough in their friendship to write frankly to Mrs Butler[39] that she ought to leave her other philanthropic work to those most suited to it and to concentrate all her own efforts to obtaining political power for women. In a rare insight into her appreciation of personal and feminine things, Lydia wrote thanking Mrs Butler for 'the beauty and richness of your gifts . . . they are lovely and seemed to bring an atmosphere of your presence with them'. She was particularly delighted with a bonnet which suited her perfectly and she wished that her friend could come and see her in it.

It is an indication of the importance that she attached to these exchanged intimacies that she could always find time, amid all the pressures of public life and in spite of indifferent health and constant weariness, to maintain her correspondence. In the years to come her commitments at both local and national level placed a very heavy load upon her frail shoulders and the affectionate interchange of letters with friends who understood and supported her gave her the sympathetic encouragement which enabled her to go on.

Chapter 6

CONSIDERING the strength of the opposition to giving women the parliamentary vote and the strong passions which the subject aroused, it was amazing that, in 1869, the municipal franchise should have been extended to women with barely a voice raised in dissent. It was a vindication of Lydia Becker's repeated assertion that, because in earlier days women ratepayers had participated in municipal elections until that right was removed by the Municipal Corporations Act of 1835, it was the restoration of women's rights that was at issue in the Municipal Franchise Bill, and not a demand for something hitherto unheard of.

The Bill had been introduced in the spring of 1869 as a result of the investigations of a Select Committee into corrupt practices in municipal elections and it set out to give the vote to every *male* occupier of a house who had resided in the borough for at least a year. Jacob Bright was able to persuade the Bill's sponsor, his friend and near neighbour John Hibbert, the member for Oldham, to agree to an amendment to omit the word *male*, and this was moved by Jacob Bright at the committee stage. Lydia confided her optimism to Jessie Boucherett in a letter dated 3rd May 1869:

> I feel quite encouraged, for I really think it may be carried. It will be a grand step towards the Parliamentary franchise.

She was prepared to take a deputation to the House of Commons to lobby if necessary, but when the Home Secretary gave the amendment his full support, it was passed without a dissentient voice. Reporting the event to Barbara Bodichon, Lydia wrote that Jacob Bright's success had caused 'surprise and excitement of a quiet sort and much pleasure to real friends of the Cause'. The House had been quite full at the time and the front benches were fully occupied. So the Bill in its amended form had survived the Commons, but there was still an uneasy suspicion that it might come to grief in the Lords. Lydia was determined that nothing should stop its progress now and in June 1869 she wrote to the Marquis of Salisbury and other influential members of the upper House urging them to support the measure. But the Bill met with no opposition in the Lords and in June 1869 it passed into law. For parliamentarians concerned with formulating national and international policies, local government was seen as mere municipal housekeeping and they condescendingly admitted that women might have a role to play in this. Even the *Anti-Suffrage Review*[40], a belated convert to giving women the municipal franchise, later admitted that women were able to tackle the 'domestic work of the nation' effectively and, during the Lords' debate, the Earl of Kimberley had reassured the House that the issue had nothing to do with the parliamentary franchise.[41] By allowing women to participate in local government elections, honourable members thought they could take the heat out of the campaign for parliamentary suffrage and no one in Parliament at that time seemed to view the women's victory as the thin end of the wedge, although Lydia and her co-workers certainly saw their achievement in that light and took heart from this small victory. 'It rests with women', said Lydia, 'to pursue the advantage that has been won, and to advance from the position that has been conceded to them in local representation to that which is the goal of our efforts – the concession of the right to a share in the representation of our common country'.[42]

The success of the Municipal Franchise Bill was a cause for rejoicing but not for complacency and Lydia immediately took steps to consolidate the gain by ensuring that women were fully aware of their new rights and encouraging them to use their votes as soon as a local election occurred. At election time she embarked upon a series of speaking engagements, moving from one town to the next, from Temperance Hall to Memorial Institute, with a punishing programme of meetings on successive days wherever a municipal contest was to be held. Her audiences were lectured on the duties and responsibilities that accompanied the franchise. Politically she remained strictly impartial and neutral and never spoke in favour of any particular candidate; indeed, she deplored the intrusion of party politics into local government and believed that individuals should be judged on their personal merits. Her sole aim and purpose was to set women thinking about the kind of issues which were at stake in local elections and to encourage them to question the candidates to find out where they stood on particular questions locally and, of course, to seek their views on parliamentary suffrage for women. She wanted women to make independent decisions as to whom they wanted to see in power in their own town halls, and not to be influenced by the way in which their husbands traditionally voted.

She would often send a circular letter to every female elector in a borough, urging her to use her vote, and to use it wisely and intelligently. Being an extremely practical woman herself she was aware that to attend a polling station for the first time, possibly as an object of curiosity and even ridicule, would be an ordeal in itself especially as municipal elections tended to be rowdy affairs, and so she gave the women precise instructions for recording their votes lest they should feel ill at ease and unfamiliar with the procedure. She would explain in the clearest possible terms that each voter had, say, six votes, one for each councillor, and they must not give more than one vote per man, or vote for more than six, and the vote must be made with a cross and not with initials. She urged women to show their eagerness to vote by going early to the poll and not waiting to be taken by agents. Lydia wanted them to set the men a good example in

public spiritedness but, mindful of the masculine jibes and criticism which might be levelled against them that they were neglecting their domestic duties, she added that women voters should only go to the poll as soon as they had finished their household chores!

During the 1870s the Manchester National Society for Women's Suffrage regularly sent out printed questionnaires to every town clerk in the country requesting them to make a return of the total number of electors on their municipal registers, the number of women on the same register, the total number who voted and the number of women who voted. Of course, not every town clerk was disposed to reply, but there was a representative response which enabled the Society to prepare impressive statistics which it presented to influential people to show that women were taking their new commitment seriously and a high proportion were exercising their right to vote in a responsible and public-spirited manner. This was valuable ammunition against those who argued that women were incapable of voting independently of their husbands. Speaking on the subject of the rights and duties of women in local government at a conference on parliamentary suffrage held in Bristol in January 1879 Lydia said:

> We urge women . . . to take an interest in the local affairs in which they have a legal right to be represented, to make their votes felt as a power which must be recognised by all who would govern such affairs . . .[42]

Once women had achieved the right to vote in municipal elections the next step was to encourage their active participation in local government. At parochial level women could be churchwardens, overseers, waywardens or surveyors of roads, guardians, parish clerks and sextons. Although these offices were usually filled by men there was nothing to prevent the appointment of a woman and Lydia was at pains to make it widely known that the requirement to assemble in a parish vestry once a year in Easter week for the election of overseers and the imposition of rates 'is laid on all inhabitant ratepayers, without mention of sex. There is no doubt that women ratepayers are summoned equally with men, and that they may attend and vote'. She was particularly anxious to impress upon women that, at parochial elections of churchwardens and other officials, female ratepayers had equal rights with men and she urged women to assert their rights by taking part in elections wherever practicable:

Thus Tuesday in Easter week would in parishes become what the first of November is in boroughs, a day when thousands of women in different parts of England may be seen taking part in public affairs, forming a demonstration of women electors, and giving a practical proof that women desire and care for the suffrage.

In the same address in Bristol she told the story of a widow who had been appointed waywarden of a parish in Westmorland. This lady had complained to the surveyor about the state of the roads and, at the next election, he prevailed upon the ratepayers to elect her to the office. Perhaps he hoped that she would decline to serve and render herself liable to a fine for refusal. But the lady was equal to the occasion. She accepted the duties imposed upon her, and being of ample means, she was able to employ a clerk to assist her, and carried out a very thorough supervision of the work, making some important and alarming discoveries as to the state of the accounts.

Lydia made a careful study of various acts of Parliament to see whether any interpretation could be found which would allow women to participate in local government beyond parish level. She was forced to conclude that the Municipal Corporations Act originally applied to men only and that the extension in 1869 only gave voting rights to women, so that they were not eligible for election to town councils, but she nevertheless believed that there was nothing to prevent women from becoming members of local Boards of Health. She drew attention to a clause in the Public Health Act of 1848 in which, she said 'to use the clumsy and ungrammatical phraseology of our legislators, words importing

the masculine gender are deemed and taken to include females'. And she continued:

I cannot help thinking that some of the energy which is successful in keeping the insides of our homes clean and well ordered might usefully be extended to the care of the outside arrangements for the same end.

Although some of the legislation was ambiguous and open to more than one interpretation, there could be no doubts concerning the Elementary Education Act of 1870 which included women in all its provisions. The Act was important because it laid the foundations for the first national system of mass elementary school education, paid for partly out of the rates and partly by grants from central government. Prior to 1870 voluntary education had been in the hands of the churches, with considerable denominational rivalry between Anglicans and Nonconformists. Under the new Act these schools were allowed to continue, but where church schools did not exist or were not adequate, boroughs were empowered to set up School Boards and to levy a rate to pay for them. The schools established in this way, Board Schools as they came to be known, gave religious instruction but they were undenominational and allowed both churchgoers and non-churchgoers to obtain an elementary education for their children. For women the provisions of the Act offered both opportunity and challenge and feminists seized their chance to become involved in practical public work at local level. Not only could women vote for members of School Boards, they also had the right to serve on those Boards themselves and to be elected to any official position, whether as chairman, vicechairman or clerk. Despite the heavy demands of her suffrage work Lydia Becker could not resist such a challenge which was to her a vindication of the equality of the sexes to which her life's work was devoted. She stood as an independent candidate for the first Manchester School Board and was the first woman in the country to be elected, receiving over fifteen thousand votes, an eloquent testimony to the high regard in which she was held in her native town. There were forty-four candidates at the first election, of whom only fifteen were elected to serve. She was returned at every subsequent election and by 1882 her vote had risen to well over twenty-seven thousand. She served on the Board continuously until her death. These elections were always hotly contested and the canvassers reported that Lydia had a great following among the working classes who liked her sincere and down to earth manner of speaking. It was said that working men always kept some of their votes for Lydia and on one occasion she received so many votes that she commented amid laughter that she was far more 'the representative for Manchester than any of the members of Parliament' because far more electors had voted for her than for any of them.

Lydia was always an active and tireless member of the Board and took her duties very seriously. It irked her that her suffrage commitments frequently took her to London and elsewhere so that she was forced to send her apologies to meetings of the School Board and she longed for the day when she would see 'the Suffrage out of the way', as she expressed it, so that she could devote more time and energy to educational matters. Indeed, to look at her diary of speaking engagements throughout the seventies, to read her published papers and voluminous correspondence, it is amazing that she found the time to be so actively involved with the progress of the Manchester schools and to take such a close personal interest in many of the pupils. It was typical of the genuine concern which she felt for the children that, when a certain boy, Thomas Gleave, was brought before the magistrates for non-attendance at Ardwick Industrial School, she accompanied the lad and his mother to court and argued that the beadle, James Power, a noted despot, had used undue severity in apprehending the boy. She felt that mother and boy had not been able to state their case fully before the magistrate and, although she lost the argument in this particular instance, it was just one example of the care and attention that she gave to any possible case of unfair treatment.

From the outset the Manchester School Board was one of the most progressive in the country. At its inaugural meeting in 1870 it was agreed to admit the press to all its meetings although there was no statutory obligation to do so, but the committee felt that it should be democratically accountable and that their deliberations and decisions should be made known to the public. The Board divided Manchester into five districts and the fifteen members were each allocated to a small sub-committee of three, each with a special responsibility for one area. Each sub-committee was deputed to survey its area, to seek out all families with children under thirteen and to ensure their attendance at school. They had to establish contact with existing day schools, Sunday schools and ragged schools to discover any potential areas of co-operation, they had to look out for suitable sites or premises for new Board schools and negotiate the transfer of any existing schools to the Board. There was a tremendous amount of spadework to be done in the early years and membership of the Board was no sinecure but represented a considerable commitment in time and energy.

The Manchester Board had a very active policy in opening new schools and was a pioneer in the development of Higher Grade and Advanced Evening Schools. Lydia Becker was frequently called upon to lay a foundation stone, perform an opening ceremony or distribute prizes and she always used the occasion to expound her views on education and the equality of the sexes. When laying the memorial stone of a new school for girls and infants at Harpurhey she commented that it was the first occasion that a woman had been so honoured in the city and she was particularly pleased to be associated with a new school for girls because she believed that girls should have the same opportunities for education as boys. She thought that, the more the intellectual faculties were developed, the more effective would individuals be in any walk of life. She quoted a comment made to her by an Oxford don – 'If all this education goes on, who will wash my shirts?' – but she believed that a well-education woman, particularly if she had an elementary knowledge of chemistry, would wash shirts more effectively than an ignorant, slovenly woman. She did not agree that domestic duties should be restricted to women only and, possibly with her own home responsibilities in mind, said that, if she had her way, every boy should be taught to 'darn his own socks and cook his own chops'.[43]

At a prize-giving at Lindley Mechanics' Institution she was saddened to learn that she would not be presenting any prizes to girls, and was not convinced by the principal's explanation that girls were not admitted as pupils because it was a very rough area and students might misbehave themselves. She made caustic comment upon this in her address and, looking round her audience, observed that she could not see 'any symptoms of that terrible disease of misbehaviour which might render it unsafe for their sisters and friends to join in their classes' and she expressed the hope that girls would be allowed to study alongside the boys because a girl 'would cook her dinner all the better for understanding something of the principles of chemistry' and 'when she wanted to cut out a garment, she would certainly do it more economically if she understood principles of geometry'. She wanted everyone to be given the opportunity to cultivate a love of beauty and her audience responded with laughter and cheers when she observed that 'if there were more art culture amongst women, we might see something of the monstrosities of dress disappear'. Although conservative in her own manner of dress, she was not prudish in disapproving of finery, but believed that decoration in women's dress should not be over-elaborate and should always be combined with good taste.[43]

Compulsory education for every child was a novel concept and by no means universally welcomed and at first Lydia had to cope with a great deal of apathy and even antagonism among parents in her district. She was quick to recognise that parents had been placed in a dilemma; as the eldest child of a large family herself she knew that older children were frequently expected to take charge of the little ones and, in poor families, they took their turn in cleaning and shopping as well. Many of them were working part-time in the mills and could earn a valuable half crown a week to augment the meagre family income, so parents were unlikely to welcome the idea of compulsory school attendance. The School Board was forced to recognise that the regulation was virtually unworkable and, in 1871, a system of half-time education was set up as a practical expedient, allowing children between the ages of eight and thirteen to work a factory shift from six in the morning to twelve noon, or from one o'clock to six in the evening, and to attend school for the other half of the day, although it is doubtful that they were able to do justice to either, with no time for relaxation, play, or even sufficient sleep for growing children. One of Lydia's tasks was to visit homes and investigate cases of non-attendance. If a child's earnings were all that stood between a family and destitution she had the utmost sympathy for a parent who might otherwise be thrown upon the parish, but if she felt that the child's earnings were a mere indulgence to be squandered by the father in the public house, then she could be a most stern disciplinarian. She had the power to make fathers responsible for the education of their children but she wished she had the power to make them responsible for feeding and clothing them. 'No child', she said, 'should be starved by its parents either physically or mentally'.

The School Board was particularly concerned about the special needs of children who sold newspapers throughout the city in the latter part of every day, and they tried to open a morning school for them but were refused a permit by the Department of Education. So important did they feel this project to be, they went ahead in defiance of the Department's decision but, after struggling for three months, they were forced to abandon the scheme for lack of funds as no government grants were forthcoming. They did, however, endeavour to do everything in their power to assist destitute children and in 1874 the Manchester School Board paid out the highest sum of any Board in the country towards the fees of poor children; a massive £2,405 was allocated compared with £824 in Liverpool and £143 in Sheffield. They were well in advance of their time too in the provision of free school meals and in a single four month period some 63,000 breakfasts and 40,000 dinners had been served regularly to 1500 children who would otherwise not have eaten before going to school.

Lydia Becker was not only active in committee and an important influence in the decision making process, she also spoke with the authority of one who visited schools regularly and knew their problems and difficulties at first hand. She was frequently to be seen doing the rounds of the schools in her area and on one occasion, at Lombard Street school, she unwittingly caused a furore by commenting upon the gloomy and frightening nature of the religious pictures or texts which were displayed round the walls. Her remarks were made in a private conversation with the principal as she was being shown round the classroom, but her words were overheard and reported to a local alderman who, perhaps because he disapproved of her feminist views and her female influence in public affairs, made a great issue of an essentially trivial matter, accusing her of wounding people's religious susceptibilities, so that she felt obliged to defend herself by writing to the newspapers:

. . . I never attempted to interfere, nor do I consider that I have any right to interfere, with the decorations of the school.

She noted that her comments had been made in private and reported by an eavesdropper, and remarked drily that if the spirit of the motto 'God is love' was not only up on the walls but spread abroad in people's hearts, it would be better for everyone and such unpleasant incidents would not arise.[44]

Lydia enjoyed her school visits and it gave her great pleasure to watch children happily at work. She criticised the compulsory practice of teaching girls to sew in elementary schools, believing that this was a skill which could be acquired outside the classroom, and felt that it was far more important 'that a mother should know how to keep her child alive and well than be able to make it a frock'. It gave her satisfaction to see girls handling dolls and learning something about basic child care, having been deeply shocked to hear of a woman feeding her four-month old baby on beer, bacon, potatoes and pastry and she knew that there was great ignorance and prejudice among working class women which only education would overcome.

The shortage of teachers worried and upset her and she dreaded that a school might have to close for lack of staff. She felt most strongly that education should not depend upon voluntary effort but that 'all teachers should be paid and well paid too'. No child should have to rely upon the chance contributions of the charitably disposed, but teachers should be officers of the state with good salaries. The disparity in pay between men and women teachers aroused her wrath:

Why should the pay of a schoolmistress be less than that of a schoolmaster, when the education required and the work demanded is the same?

Women should have the right to compete freely for all educational positions:

If a woman teacher can be had equally efficient with a man for three-fourths of the salary, why are not these efficient teachers allowed to compete freely for all educational posts, and why do they not displace the schoolmasters, which would be the case if the law of supply and demand were allowed free play? The answer is, that it is arbitrarily assumed that women cannot teach boys, and therefore they are shut out from the most profitable part of the teaching profession. If, after a fair trial, it had been found that women were incompetent to teach boys up to the age of thirteen years, which is the age at which they cease to attend the elementary schools, no complaint would be made; but women have some reason to complain that they are excluded from these posts without any trial. Experience seems to prove that women make excellent teachers of boys.[45]

In the early years of the School Boards this was a contentious question. Although in Scotland it was the universal practice for women to teach boys, and prevailed to some extent in England, there was a tendency for male teachers to resist what they saw as the 'encroachment' of women into the profession. In 1879 the Birmingham Education Authority was forced to abandon its policy of allowing women to teach boys after the men had protested that it was 'an encouragement to immorality' but Lydia saw no reason why women should not teach boys up to the age of thirteen.

During her long association with the School Board Lydia Becker won the confidence of parents and was a popular figure among them. She was described as 'homely rather than beautiful' and this endeared her to many ordinary folk who found that she had a sympathetic ear for their problems and difficulties. Although she never married she had been largely responsible for the education of her younger brothers and sisters and believed firmly that school should be a happy place and that love should be the teacher's guiding principle. She once spoke somewhat disparagingly of the 'modern notions' of the Froebel system of education and she favoured learning tables by rote and constant repetition of useful formulas as the best way of teaching arithmetic. Yet she had perfected a less conventional technique within her own family for teaching the younger children to read and claimed that any child could be taught to read within six months. Her sister Esther thought it was 'a splendid method of teaching' using a phonic system and family reading lessons were 'a pleasure to teacher and taught'. In January 1859 Lydia began teaching her four year old sister Louisa to read and, by giving lessons every day, the child was reading well by the beginning of June. Lydia wrote to a friend that 'reading is everything' but 'grammar is a thing no young child should even hear of'. She thought that most English grammars were made up of pure nonsense and did nothing but confuse, but she knew the important of reading aloud to children and introducing them to good stories and pictures. She also encouraged singing and physical exercise, particularly the art of callisthenics, or learning to move gracefully.

Her overriding concern was to ensure that girls had as much opportunity for education as boys. At a prize-giving at Todmorden she was disappointed that only seven of the ninety-three students were women, she felt that this did not represent the intellectual capacity of the young women of the town, and requested that more women should be actively encouraged to join the classes. She used a sum of money sent by a friend to set up a Becker scholarship to be competed for by both boys and girls, and it gave her immense pleasure and satisfaction that it was won by a girl who eventually went on to graduate at Victoria University, which had been chartered in 1880, comprised three university colleges, at Liverpool, Manchester and Leeds, and admitted women to classes and degrees on equal terms with men. She tried to ensure that more women were appointed as officers of the School Board so that the first person a neglected child would see would be 'some kind woman it could love', and one of her last acts in connection with the Board was the appointment of a lady superintendent to supervise instruction in nursing, dressmaking, cookery and laundry in night schools.

Although Lydia's election to the Manchester School Board came at a time when her suffrage activities were at their peak, she never allowed one commitment to detract from the other even though she was frequently unwell and suffering from considerable physical strain. She had to prove to her critics that a woman could contribute conscientiously and effectively to local government if given the opportunity and, for the rest of her life, she maintained a high public profile as a member of the Board, demonstrating her intense personal interest and involvement in the schools in her care and a passionate concern for the well-being of the children for whom she was responsible.

Chapter 7

THROUGHOUT the 1860s the suffrage movement had grown in numbers and was steadily gaining momentum and women really believed that they were beginning to see some rewards for their persistent campaigning. The hitherto taboo subject of votes for women had been given a place on the parliamentary agenda and Members of Parliament had been forced to confront the issue for the first time as a matter of serious debate, not to be trivialised or dismissed with a few facetious remarks. When, in 1869, the Municipal Franchise Bill passed into law and women were at last accorded the right to participate in local government, Lydia Becker and her colleagues honestly believed that the battle was almost won and that it needed but one last concerted effort for victory to be theirs. Many suffrage societies had come into being up and down the country but it was still a fragmented movement and, in the conviction that strength lies in unity, Lydia's vision was to bring the disparate groups together as a single, cohesive, powerful whole. Her success in initiating the National Society for Women's Suffrage was an important step forward, the next logical development was to give the movement a medium of communication and she conceived the idea of a monthly journal which would put women in touch with each other and keep them informed of all that was happening, both regionally and at a national level.

In March 1870 the *Journal of the Manchester National Society for Women's Suffrage* was launched by the Manchester Executive Committee with Lydia Becker as editor. In her first editorial Lydia wrote that the object of the Journal was 'to extend to every isolated well-wisher the firm grasp of an outstretched hand' and she repeated her personal conviction that isolation is a cause of weakness and that no one can work well without sympathy and encouragement from others who are like-minded. From the outset the Journal aimed at a national readership and the first issue carried reports of public meetings as far apart as Edinburgh and Bath, Newcastle and Crewe, Bristol and South Shields. Much space was devoted to detailed coverage of parliamentary debates and the division lists were always printed so that readers could see for themselves how their own Member of Parliament had voted.

The Journal bore all the hallmarks of Lydia's personality. It was produced with a degree of professionalism which would have done credit to any national newspaper and her forthright style and meticulous attention to accuracy and detail were evident in every issue. Press reviews of the new periodical praised it for being 'well-written and conducted with great spirit and enterprise' and it was commended as 'a popular upholder of women's rights' and 'a clever advocate of the movement reflecting much credit on the editorship'. The Journal was modestly priced at one penny and throughout its twenty years the price was never increased. The monthly issues were cumulated into annual volumes, bound in a green paper cover and sold for one shilling and sixpence.

The favourable press reviews were gratifying to Lydia because they encouraged subscribers and it was vital to build up a substantial subscription list to ensure a regular income. She determined from the outset that the Journal must be self-supporting and could not be a drain upon the limited funds of the Manchester National Society. The sixteen page periodical was closely set, with fairly narrow margins and no illustrations, very typical of newspapers of the period, and it must have involved a considerable amount of typesetting and proofing. A printer's estimate found among Lydia's papers quoted the sum of

£17 5s. 0d. to print five thousand copies and £2 3s. 0d. for each additional thousand. It is not clear whether this was the accepted quotation but it gives some idea of the production costs and demonstrates the need for Lydia to maintain a high circulation if she was to break even. The price of one penny could have allowed very little for overheads, especially as the Journal was placed free of charge in many institutions and sent to every member of both Houses of Parliament.

Within a year the title of the periodical had changed and it had become the *Women's Suffrage Journal*; it had divorced itself from the Manchester Society and had become a fully national journal. It had established a reputation for quality and the first commercial advertiser had been persuaded to take a regular full page display advertisement for the Willcox and Gibbs sewing machine. In 1874 the Journal appeared in a permanently enlarged form and a number of small display advertisements began to appear, for Epp's Cocoa, Yorkshire Relish and Goodall's Baking-powder ('the best penny packet in the world') and by 1877 the regular readership was so assured that the paper attracted such nationally well known products as Reckitts Blue and Bengers Food. At the same time the editorial was moved off the front page, which then became nominally a contents page, but in fact consisted mainly of a large number of small classified advertisements which again would have been a useful source of revenue. It is interesting to speculate how many of the Journal's advertisers took space purely for commercial reasons, seeing the predominantly female readership as a potential market for their domestic wares, or how many were prompted by higher motives and were, in fact, using advertising as a way of sponsoring the movement and supporting it with regular financial contributions.

Lydia used a variety of editorial ploys to hold her readers; in 1880 she inaugurated a monthly *Calendar*, not the usual diary of forthcoming events, but more akin to an almanac, listing the phases of the sun and moon and showing only those dates and anniversaries which were significant to the women's struggle – the beginning of the new Lent term at Girton College, a new charter admitting women to degrees in the University of London, the anniversary of the founding of the Victoria Press, a printing business run by trained women compositors, which within three years had received the accolade of Printer and Publisher in Ordinary to Her Majesty. Later on prize competitions became a regular feature, five shillings being awarded to the successful entrant and results published in the magazine the following month. One such competition was for the best anagram composed from the letters in the sentence 'The nineteenth century ladies who do not want to vote' and this was won by the historian of the early suffrage movement, Helen Blackburn[46], with the entry 'Denote when counted a very thin total, then 'tis too new' and the runner-up, whose pseudonym *Bodon* seems to be but a light disguise for the spirited Barbara Bodichon submitted the more forthright 'The worthy inane noodles that veto it we needn't count'.

Although the Journal had its lighter side, its main purpose was always to disseminate information and this it did supremely well. Parliamentary activities were meticulously reported and in great detail. The complete text of any relevant Bill would be printed, followed by the full debate in the House and the division lists. Speeches by Members of Parliament, whether in the House or elsewhere were comprehensively reported and letters from them to their constituents or the editor printed. Individual suffrage societies sent in reports of their meetings and regular coverage was given to lectures, public meetings and all speeches by members of the National Society for Women's Suffrage. There was always a selection of reviews, correspondence and extracts from the national press.

The Journal did not confine itself to the suffrage; its coverage was wide-ranging and any subject which touched upon women and their rights was grist to its mill. On one occasion, under the headline 'Shocking treatment of a wife' the paper reported how a husband had set his bulldog at his wife, inciting it to bite her while he continued to hit and kick the woman. He had received a six months' sentence and Lydia commented:

> We presume that at the expiration of his sentence, Mr Bradley will have the legal right to compel his wife to live with him and his bulldog, if she should be fortunate or unfortunate enough to survive for such a fate.

She publicised the tragic story of the deaths of a mother and baby from starvation in the workhouse; the mother so lacked nourishment herself that she was unable to feed her baby. She followed up a story in *The Lancet* in 1871 which had told how a coroner had ordered a physical examination of a woman in a case of suspected infanticide and concealment of birth. This was topical because in 1870, amid a storm of hostility, Josephine Butler had begun her crusade to secure the repeal of the Contagious Diseases Acts. It was a protest against existing laws concerning the regulation of prostitutes which gave powers to the police to declare any woman living in a certain area – a garrison town for example – a common prostitute and, as such, bound to submit to periodic medical examination, with refusal punishable by imprisonment. By 1871, when Lydia highlighted this individual case in the Journal, a Royal Commission had investigated the Acts and come out unanimously in favour of immediate discontinuance of compulsory medical examinations and Lydia, together with a Manchester colleague Elizabeth Wolstenholme,[47] supported Josephine Butler in setting up a committee to raise funds to enable them to challenge such cases of 'illegal outrage' in the courts. They attacked both the Home Secretary and the Lord Chancellor on the subject without getting a satisfactory reply and they made it known to the medical profession that they would proceed against any one who became involved in this grossly illegal practice.

Discrimination in employment was a frequent topic for comment and discussion. In the first few months of its life the Journal published a table showing the respective wages paid to men and women in one Lancashire mill in June 1870. Although nearly two thirds of the wealth of the cotton manufacturing industry was generated by the labour of women, they were consistently paid less than the men for identical jobs. The mill employed two hundred women and only seventy eight men and a female weaver earned thirteen shillings and five pence a week, compared to over sixteen shillings for a man. For card-room hands the differential was even greater, the men earning nearly six shillings a week more than the women. It was not only the differences in pay that aroused Lydia's wrath. She was vehemently opposed to the Nine Hours Factory Bill which would make it an offence for women to earn money during more than nine hours a day, whereas they had previously been allowed to work for ten. Although Lydia might have been expected to favour a reduction in women's working hours, she argued, no doubt correctly, that they could not afford to have their wages diminished and would overstrain themselves in order to maintain the same level of production in a shorter working day:

> In these things it is the pace that kills, and it may well be that a decrease in the total number of hours of work may be more than counterbalanced by the greater strain during working hours, and the prolongation of the time of continuous labour without refreshment or rest . . . Mr Mundella's Bill allows one hour for dinner, and it is intended that no other meal shall be taken during the nine hours' working day. A Scotch [sic] working man gets two meals and two hours of time out of his work hours. An Englishwoman, even if she is a nursing mother, is to have only one meal and one hour of rest during the whole of her outdoor working day.

She went on to make the point that a man had only to get up, have breakfast and go to work and then return home to find a meal on the table and the rest of the evening his own, but for the woman:

> It may be fairly said that she is working in some way or other from rising in the morning

until going to rest at night. Such is the routine prescribed by law and custom for what is called the weaker sex. 'All work and no play' may be a bad thing for Jack, but it is considered the right thing for Jack's mother; and men are asking Parliament to limit the hours of women's remunerative labour in order that they may have more time, not for 'play', but for domestic work.[48]

In December 1870 Lydia drew her readers' attention to the plight of women farmers who were denied membership of the Royal Agricultural Society which would have given them access to the same benefits and privileges as their male counterparts – members were entitled to advantageous terms for feeding stuffs and to free soil examinations – and even when a competition for the best managed farm was won by a woman, she was still not admitted into membership. Two years later controversy raged round the employment of women in the Civil Service and there was a public outcry when the Postmaster General allowed female clerks to be on the establishment of the Post Office Savings Bank. In 1872 the Journal compared the inferior status of working Englishwomen with female printers in France where the Didot family firm of learned printers and publishers employed an almost exclusively female workforce for its specialised books which included an encyclopedia and an *Annuaire de Commerce*. The firm was noted for its typographical perfection and women undertook all the skilled work, including reading and composing in French, Latin and Greek. Any unusual story of women's skill and courage was avidly reported. Under the headline *Woman as Navigator* the story was told of the death of a ship's master, his first mate and the leading seaman from yellow fever while the ship was on the high seas and how the master's wife was the only person left on board sufficiently skilled in the arts of navigation to bring the ship safely to port.

Occasionally Lydia used the Journal to ride her own hobbyhorses. She had once, at the British Association Congress in Newcastle in 1889, replied to Mrs Stopes'[49] denunciation of restrictive female support garments and declared herself 'an out and out defender of the corsets' considering them 'absolutely necessary for the health, comfort, and appearance of women'. Her personal enthusiasm was no doubt due to the chronic weakness in her own back and her need for some surgical support and she returned to the subject again in an article for the *Sanitary Record* and also in the Journal where she reported to her satisfaction that:

A new benefit of corsets is shown by the incidents of a trial for attempted murder at the last Manchester Assizes. The man tried to shoot his wife with a pistol. The bullet entered her back, but her corsets prevented it from entering her chest and killing her.[50]

In November 1889, at the sale of work following the annual general meeting of the Manchester National Society for Women's Suffrage, one of the objects exhibited was a pair of corsets sent to Lydia by an enthusiastic manufacturer in Vienna in recognition of her defence of the use of such garments.

The *Women's Suffrage Journal* had many contributors and reporters who sent in news and reports from all parts of the country and the world. Articles on municipal suffrage in Canada, Russian women students, civil rights in Russia and women's rights in Italy appeared alongside excerpts from *Hansard* and reports of public meetings from Southampton to Edinburgh. But it was Lydia's editorial direction which stamped the Journal with her own inimitable style. She gave free rein to her journalistic aspirations in her leading articles which were models of plain speaking and good common sense. In July 1870 the Journal reported in full the debate in the House of Commons on the motion to allow the Women's Disabilities Bill to go into committee. One opponent of the Bill had said that, if the House yielded to women's demands 'it would be as if the Knight of La Mancha, the impersonation of chivalrous regard for women, had desired to reduce Dulcinea to the level of an ordinary mortal'. In her editorial Lydia condemned such sentimental objections to the Bill and took up the Don Quixote theme and turned it to her own advantage:

> If we remember rightly the story of the Knight of La Mancha, the fair Dulcinea was in fact a washerwoman, and we think that if she had put in a claim for an advance of wages, an extra bunch of garlic for her pottage, or even as an aid to the amelioration of her lot, for such a modicum of political privilege as the constitution of Spain accorded to Sancho Panza, it would have been a very unsatisfactory reply if she had been told that to grant her demands would reduce her to the level of an ordinary mortal, and that chivalrous regard for women forbade that she should be taken down from the high pedestal on which she was placed. To us it appears that the notions regarding women entertained by the opponents of the Bill resembled very closely those of the Knight of La Mancha. They decline to regard women as ordinary mortals, they place them on an ideal pedestal, invest them with imaginary attributes, and base their arguments on the assumption that women are exempted from the rough trials and burdens of life. They refuse to recognise the real Dulcinea at her wash-tub, they see only the ideal creation of the crazy knight's disordered brain.[51]

For twenty years Lydia maintained this incredible journalistic output, always writing under great pressure to meet her monthly deadlines, and still managing to combine her editorial responsibilities with all her other commitments to the local and national suffrage committees and the school board, without allowing any aspect of her work to suffer. Small wonder that, when she died, her colleagues felt unequal to the task of maintaining the Journal to the high standards which she had achieved and which the readers had come to expect. In August 1890 they produced a final and memorial number which contained the material that Lydia had already prepared at the time of her death together with tributes from a number of her friends and colleagues who had known her long and well in her public work. The proprietor of the *Englishwoman's Review*, which for upwards of twenty-five years had advocated the advancement of women, entered into an agreement with the Central Committee of the National Society for Women's Suffrage and henceforth contained a section devoted to women's suffrage as the official organ of that Society. The sorrowing staff of the *Women's Suffrage Journal* sent this message to all its readers:

> For twenty years and four months this journal has received the impress of one hand and one mind, so that its long row of volumes form one continuous work, and now when that careful hand is laid low and the energies of that farseeing mind are carried beyond our mortal ken, it would seem fitting to close these pages where Miss Becker left them, that so the Journal shall be wholly hers, nor suffer by any change to any less experienced hand or any mind less comprehensive.[52]

Chapter 8

MOST people would regard the editorship of a national journal as a full time occupation in itself, but Lydia managed to combine her writing with a constant stream of other activities. As secretary of the Manchester Society she was the driving force of the organisation, perpetually arranging public meetings and fund-raising events and, because she was so much identified with the movement, she was much in demand as a speaker whenever a suffrage meeting was arranged.

In 1873 the Becker family kept a communal diary in which all their comings and goings were recorded and it shows Lydia to have been away from Manchester for about ninety days of the year. Every single month, from January to June, she was travelling the north of England, besides fitting in visits to Oxford and London, but just when one might have expected her to take a well earned summer break she was off to Blackpool on 29th July at the start of a lecture tour, not returning home until 16th August, from the Lake District. The following day she was at Alderley, no doubt reporting back to Jacob Bright and his wife, and three days later she set out for Chester and North Wales to arrange a series of meetings, returning to Manchester on the 23rd. After a few days at home she was off again to address meetings in Matlock and Buxton and was only back with the family for one night before leaving for the lecture tour in North Wales which lasted a week. She came home on 9th September and went the following day to Harrogate. On 17th September she was in Bradford for the British Association meeting, not returning home until the 27th and leaving again on 1st October for Saltburn on Sea. With such a punishing schedule it is small wonder that she once had cause to complain to a friend that she had absolutely no time to think about replenishing her wardrobe!

By the 1870s support for the suffrage movement had reached a peak. A public meeting in Manchester's Free Trade Hall presided over by Jacob Bright in 1874 was 'crowded to overflowing with an interested and sympathetic audience' which encouraged the Committee to plan a further twenty-three meetings in places as diverse as Sheffield and Caernarvon, Northampton and Nottingham. A special fund was set up to enable Lydia to visit holiday resorts at the height of the summer season, in July and August, for the purpose of attracting visitors to her lectures, on the principle that the holidaymakers had come from all parts of the country and would carry her message back home when they dispersed. And so, while most people were enjoying a well-earned rest, Lydia was busy drumming up support for The Cause in Llandudno, Rhyl, Saltburn, Redcar and Harrogate.

In 1877 Jacob Bright was back in Parliament and another bill was set down for 6th June, preceded by a whole series of public meetings and petitions. On the day before the debate Lydia was one of a deputation, led by Lady Anne Gore–Langton,[53] to the Chancellor of the Exchequer, Sir Stafford Northcote. He gave them a courteous hearing, but if he encouraged them by declaring that he was not opposed to women's suffrage in principle, he disappointed them with his final remarks:

> It resolves itself with me into a question of time and expediency; and I am bound to say, speaking quite frankly, that I do not think the present a particularly desirable time for reopening the great electoral question.

Despite the Chancellor's equivocation, the women had many promises of support among Members of Parliament and they filled the ladies' gallery in optimistic mood. But the debate took an unexpected turn, graphically described by Helen Blackburn:

Mr Courtney[54] had risen at 5.15 to reply to Mr Butt, when the Opposition burst into a tumultuous uproar, which effectually prevented his words from being heard. When it became apparent that the opponents would not listen to arguments, the purpose was formed amongst the Members on the side of the Bill to prevent a vote being taken, and Mr Courtney breasted the storm of yells and cries that drowned his voice until the clock struck the hour of closing.

Those wild notes, *Divide! divide!! divide!!!* came surging up in boisterous billows of sound to the ladies' gallery, and struck on the ears of the listeners there in painful discord with the earnest yearning with which they regarded what to them was a holy cause. Truly the echoes of that afternoon ring even now in one's memory as the most painful experience of all those years.[55]

In the light of this fiasco Lady Anne Gore–Langton called a meeting at her London home in Hanover Square and Lydia was invited to speak. The scene in the House of Commons had only strengthened the movement's resolve and one speaker, Mrs William Grey, who had hitherto been active in education but admitted her indifference to the suffrage, forcefully expressed the view that they would never get justice in education or any other field without the suffrage and concluded 'I wish all thrown into the women's suffrage scale.'

Plate 7. Lydia Becker at a women's rights meeting at Hanover Square Rooms, London, 1872.

45

Parliament was dissolved in March 1880 and, in anticipation of a change in government, the biggest suffrage event was a grand National Demonstration of Women, once again held in the Free Trade Hall, and the principal motive of the organisers was to test the reality of the alleged demand for women's suffrage. They figured that if thousands of women came together attracted, not by any great names, but simply and solely by their presence to manifest their support and sympathy, that would be a testimony to the strength and popularity of the movement which could not be explained away. The scene in the Free Trade Hall that evening drew the opening remark from the president, Priscilla McLaren,[56] 'Is this a dream or reality?' for the whole vast area, galleries and platform, was thronged with a dense crowd composed, with the exception of reporters, exclusively of women. Many filled the precincts and could not gain admission and an overflow meeting was quickly arranged in the Memorial Hall. Lydia said it was a marvellous meeting, grand in numbers and fervent enthusiasm and 'gave to each a new revelation of the power of collective womanhood'.

A few months later, in the summer of 1880, a movement had begun to make itself felt in the Isle of Man to extend the franchise to all *male* householders, enabling them to vote for the ancient House of Keys. This was the signal for the ever watchful Manchester Society to move into action with a campaign urging that women's claims to the vote should also be considered. Lydia Becker and a companion, Mrs Scatcherd, were dispatched to the Island and held a series of meetings, addressing crowded audiences in Douglas, Ramsey, Peel and Castletown. It was the first time that the subject of women's suffrage had been aired in the Isle of Man and the speakers were well received wherever they went and given good press coverage. As a direct result of their intense campaigning an amendment to enfranchise women householders was brought before the House of Keys and, to everyone's astonishment and joy, carried by an overwhelming majority. The Island's Electoral Reform Act received Queen Victoria's royal assent on 5th January 1881 and the Manchester Committee ventured to suggest that the mainland's House of Commons would not be less just in its treatment of women. The first election to take place under the new Act was held in March 1881 and every one of the thousand eligible women received a letter of congratulations from Lydia Becker. On election day women voters were first at the poll in many places and were said to be 'quick, intelligent and business-like in their procedure and they always knew for whom they wished to vote'.

The campaign in the Isle of Man had been short and sharp and, to everyone's surprise, crowned with success. Soon after the initial victory the House of Keys went even further and extended the franchise to women occupiers as well as owners. Yet, in mainland Britain, private members' bills had been introduced in the House of Commons almost every year throughout the 1870s and, with monotonous regularity, were easily defeated on the second reading. Every parliamentary occasion was supported by suffrage meetings up and down the country, attracting huge numbers of enthusiastic women, and petitions were presented carrying thousands of signatures, but all this activity was clearly having very little effect at Westminster. Some suffragists laid the blame for this at the door of the Central Committee in London which, they felt, was not functioning efficiently or exerting any real influence upon Parliament. A special sub-committee was set up to look into these allegations and it was decided to appoint a new secretary, someone who would infuse new life into the organisation. The natural choice was Lydia Becker – she was already a well known and much respected figure, a competent administrator and a forceful speaker. She was seen to be the obvious person to knit the many suffrage societies together into a single, powerful organisation. Laura McLaren was entrusted with the task of sounding her out on this proposition and, in February 1881, she wrote to Lydia:

> With your intimate knowledge of the political work which lies before us, you will quickly

see all the bearings of this proposal . . . the strong feeling we all have in favour of uniting our forces under the leadership of one whose political ability and talent we have always recognised. It appears there is a waste of force in having two centres of political action, and although the energy of Manchester is powerfully felt in the country, still, as all Parliamentary business must be transacted in London, it is here we need the powerful head to act promptly . . . The movement is your pet child which you have seen grow up from infancy and whose welfare is nearest your heart.[57]

It was a major decision for Lydia to move away from Manchester where she had spent all her life but it was an offer which she could hardly refuse. She agreed initially to take the job for a trial period of one year and she was offered a salary of £200. She was to be wholly responsible for the work of the London office and, as parliamentary agent, the post required her residence in London while Parliament was in session and an exercise of supervision during the rest of year. The Committee recognised that she would still have responsibilities in Manchester which would demand her presence there for a few days every month and they were prepared to afford her every facility for this. She was allowed to engage clerical assistance for her London office and she took up her duties on 2nd April.

So began an intense period of parliamentary pressure and Lydia became a familiar and respected figure in the lobbies at Westminster. A Liberal government had been returned to power in 1880 under Gladstone and the extension of the suffrage figured prominently in their programme. With a new Reform Bill in prospect the suffragists abandoned their strategy of introducing private members' bills every year and concentrated all their efforts upon securing massive support for an amendment to the Bill itself. Lydia wrote to Mrs Ashworth Hallett on 2nd April 1880 that they should 'take advantage of the opening of the door by others to get in ourselves', and they persuaded William Woodall to agree to propose an amendment to the Bill

that 'words importing the masculine gender should include women'.

Between 1880 and 1884 there were nine huge demonstrations by women in London and other key cities and, in every case, the largest available hall was filled to overflowing with women of all ranks and occupations, with men consigned to the galleries as mere spectators. In Manchester Lydia had been much encouraged by a meeting she had organised in October 1879 which had attracted hundreds of women. 'How they listened – how they cheered' she wrote to Priscilla McLaren, 'how strong and intelligent an interest they took in what was said to them. It would have done your heart good to see!'. The strength and optimism engendered by that meeting emboldened her to take the Free Trade Hall in February of the following year. Several days before the event she began to have cold feet and enquired whether a portion of the hall could be partitioned off if it proved too large. Her fears were ungrounded – the hall was packed and they had to make room for an overflowing meeting. At each of the nine meetings memorials to the Government were adopted unanimously.

A letter signed by many representative women of the day, including Florence Nightingale, Lady Verney, Mrs Fawcett[58] and others, was sent to every Member of Parliament and a memorial stating that no measure for the extension of the franchise would be satisfactory unless it included women, was signed by over a hundred Members of Parliament and presented to Gladstone. Adeline Paulina Irby and Sophia Jex Blake[59] wrote to *The Times* in support of William Woodall's amendment describing themselves as 'two working women, who have hitherto taken little part in the agitation' and pointing out that, as the present Bill was intended to settle the question of the franchise, at least for a generation, 'to pass it without doing justice to women' would postpone their inclusion indefinitely.[60]

William Woodall[61] moved his clause in the House on 10th June 1884 and, although both the Prime Minister and the Conservative leader, Northcote, were at pains to stress the non-party character of the amendment, it was overwhelmingly defeated after Gladstone declared his own personal opposition to it in the words:

> The cargo which the vessel carries is, in our opinion, a cargo as large as she can safely carry . . . women's suffrage would overweight the ship . . . With regard to the proposal to introduce it into this Bill, I offer it the strongest opposition in my power, and I must disclaim and renounce all responsibility for the measure should my honourable friend succeed in inducing the Committee to adopt the amendment.[62]

One hundred and four members of Parliament, mostly Liberals, had indicated in advance to the NSWS that they were in favour of the amendment and the suffragists had calculated that, if members were free to vote according to conscience, the clause would be carried by a majority of seventy-two. With such a large margin for error they were naturally euphoric, buoyed up by the considerable mass of support they had been promised and confident that this time they really would succeed. But when it came to the crucial division, members lacked the courage of their convictions and voted against Woodall's amendment rather than incur the displeasure of their leader who had made his own views known in such plain terms. This massive parliamentary defeat – two hundred and seventy one members opposed the amendment – was a crushing blow for the women campaigners. After three years' intensive lobbying and drumming up support throughout the country, they were convinced that at last Parliament was on their side and the battle all but won. The ignominious defeat highlighted the basic ineffectiveness of their strategy which had always been to influence back-benchers and win them over the The Cause, whereas they should have gone all out to convert members of the Cabinet, where the real power lay.

There was intense bitterness in the movement at what came to be called 'the great betrayal' and Frances Power Cobbe,[63] in a letter to Lydia soon after the event, echoed the feelings of all suffragists when she referred to Gladstone as 'the arch-enemy' who had been their ruin and hoped that he would be finally defeated in the next election. Even that fervent wish was not granted, and Gladstone returned in 1886 for a third term.

The suffragists had never been so dispirited although Lydia insisted that they had never been over sanguine or underrated the difficulties of the task. Feelings of despondency and futility began to infiltrate the movement and it began to lose momentum now that its political impotence was so apparent and, as enthusiasm wilted, internal divisions began to surface. Lydia had become accustomed to addressing packed audiences at all her speaking engagements but now the first signs of dwindling support began to show themselves and, although reserved seats were still filled to capacity, attendance in unreserved parts of a hall could be very scanty. The first ever petition to Parliament in 1866 had created a tremendous stir but a decade later such petitions had become commonplace and lost some of their original impact and the suffrage movement, as then constituted, was in danger of running out of steam. For many women, to be able to participate in local government and to see some of the professions being opened up to them was sufficient reward for their hard work, and they were not unduly concerned about the parliamentary franchise. Also, in the wake of the Corrupt Practices Act of 1883, canvassing and other election work ceased to be a salaried occupation reserved for men and women were welcomed into the political parties as unpaid workers, diverting the energies of hitherto active suffragists who seized this new opportunity to play a supporting role in the political parties. Women's Liberal Associations were set up in many towns and the Midland Union of Conservative Associations soon had a Ladies' Auxiliary Council. Women were more often active in public life and female speakers were no longer a novelty, guaranteed to attract a large crowd, so the suffrage societies found it more and more difficult to command public attention. They would never have considered the kind of tactics later adopted by the suffragettes of seeking publicity through confrontation with the law and their campaign thus became a tedious and repetitive treadmill of rather uninspired meetings, petitions, letters and articles in the press which rarely had anything new or original to say.

When the Central Committee met for its annual general meeting in Westminster Town Hall in July 1887 it was chaired by William Woodall who had introduced the women's suffrage amendment in Parliament three years earlier. In his address to the meeting he expressed the disillusion which was permeating the movement. Although public support for women's suffrage had grown enormously over the years, it was still the case that:

> . . . there must be a feeling of more or less depression in the minds of all present here that while the cause has undoubtedly grown in public feeling, there has been co-incidentally with this growth . . . some circumstances which seem to show that we are not very much nearer the goal . . . We feel indeed, but only in common with those who have undertaken other great reforms, the consciousness of the impotence of Parliament to give effect to the well-matured public opinion of the country.[64]

The frustration felt by the suffragists was made all the more acute in 1887 by the general rejoicing and celebrations to mark Queen Victoria's Golden Jubilee. The Queen's personal antagonism to The Cause was well known and it was perhaps with tongue in cheek that Lydia allowed herself to be one of the two leading signatories to the loyal address presented to Her Majesty by the women's suffrage societies expressing their affection and desiring

> . . . humbly to thank Your Majesty for having been graciously pleased to accord Your Royal Assent to many measures for the amelioration of the condition of the women of these realms.

However, the point was made that, although the power to elect members of the House of Commons had, during her reign, been transferred from a minority to the masses of the people, yet

> . . . in these measures the precedent of the co-equal electoral rights of men and women when similarly qualified, which is the rule in every other form of representative government in Great Britain, has not been followed, and Your Majesty's own sex are still denied the rights of citizenship and the privileges of free and constitutional government.[65]

No doubt Her Majesty was not amused to be thus reminded of her opposition to the whole concept of women's suffrage, but it was a bitter disappointment for the movement that its efforts were not to be crowned with success in this jubilee year. As William Woodall said in his chairman's address:

> It would indeed have been a very happy circumstance if we had been able to achieve this great crowning work during the Jubilee year of the Queen. We have seen how during these last fifty years . . . all the delicate organism of an intricate constitutional system has been administered with singular tact and judgement by the woman who, during all those years, has been called upon to guide, in a very large degree by her good sense and judgment, the forces of this realm . . . We have seen the great work of governing the country carried on with advantage to the country and to our time, and it would have been, as I have said, a singularly happy and appropriate celebration of the Jubilee if we had been able to remove this great and glaring disability of the sex of the Queen, which is such a strong and anomalous contradiction to the progress of the reign. However, we must be content to wait for it and to labour and do our best still further to strengthen public opinion and to bring that public opinion to bear in Parliament so that it may grant the demand.[66]

The Queen's Jubilee came and went but the goal of women's suffrage remained as remote as it had ever been. Mass support for The Cause fell away sharply, but this only stiffened the resolve of a few hardened campaigners like Lydia Becker. As inevitably happens when pressure groups begin to sense that they are fighting a lost cause, tensions and rifts began to appear and the movement, which had once been solid in its resolve, began to fragment. There were those, like the Pankhursts, who believed that the campaign should be broadened to include the vote for suitably qualified married women, and this led them to break away to form their own Women's Franchise League in 1889. Another issue which searched the National Society's conscience was its relationship with the political parties. Now that women were more politically active – in the Primrose League from 1884 and the Women's Liberal Federation from 1886 – the NSWS was faced with demands for affiliation and in 1888 this issue split the organisation down the middle and Lydia was on the verge of resignation. It was her friend Frances Power Cobbe who urged her not to resign because it would give their enemies great satisfaction if, as a result of dissension, her services were lost. In December a breakaway group calling itself the Central National Society for Women's Suffrage welcomed affiliation and took itself off to separate offices in Parliament Street while the Central Committee of the National Society for Women's Suffrage decided to remain politically neutral and Lydia, to whom this was an important principle, was re-selected as secretary. It was an unpleasant incident creating dissension and tension within a hitherto united group of women and it not only stirred up personal animosities but created a serious practical difficulty because of the significant loss of income from subscriptions. None but the few individuals intimately involved comprehended this hair-splitting move, most were thoroughly confused by the unwieldy and largely meaningless names of the two groups, and support dwindled further.

Meanwhile, in an effort to revive interest among Members of Parliament, a Parliamentary Committee was set up in 1887, chiefly at Lydia's instigation as the person most actively concerned in keeping the suffrage on the parliamentary agenda. In the general election of 1886 the number of professed supporters of The Cause to be returned to Parliament was the highest ever and, for the first time, constituted an absolute majority in the House. However, in practice, much of that support was luke-warm and not very influential, and it was an indication of the status of women within the precincts of Westminster, even after more than twenty years' campaigning, that Lydia was never admitted to the deliberations of the Parliamentary Committee but had to wait until the meetings were over when the secretaries handed their minutes to her.

For all the enthusiasm and intense publicity of the seventies and early eighties, women's suffrage remained firmly a non-party issue with neither major political party willing to espouse The Cause. Private members' bills were subject to every kind of hazard and delaying tactic and, without even the tacit approval of government, there was no hope of success. A further setback for the suffragists was the formation in 1875 of a committee 'for maintaining the integrity of the franchise'. Led by E. P. Pleydell–Bouverie, member for Kilmarnock, and supported by a group of Conservative MPs, this organisation canvassed systematically against extending the franchise to women and, to the great disadvantage of the suffragists, it numbered among its supporters several influential women, including the novelist Mrs Humphrey Ward and Beatrice Potter (later Mrs Sidney Webb). With opinion still so divided in the country it was apparent that Parliament was not ready to accede to the women's demands and no occasion for any further debate was secured until 1892, two years after Lydia's death.

Chapter 9

FOR over twenty years Lydia had worked tirelessly for women's suffrage without seeing much headway and the latter years had been marred by dissensions and divisions within the movement. She had carried much of the burden singlehanded and the strain upon her, both mental and physical, had been immense.

She had never taken a true holiday in the sense of complete relaxation. One of her fellow-workers once sent her a small gift, a cameo, from Rome, remarking in her accompanying letter that

> . . . while we go out to play, and see and think of other things, you stay at home and keep the suffrage fire ever burning.[67]

Such vacations as Lydia took were always working holidays. She was a familiar figure every year at annual meetings of the British Association, but because she was inevitably one of the speakers, it was hardly a relaxation for her although, at the end of the 1871 congress in Edinburgh she was asked if she would consent to be one of the patronesses of the closing ball. She humorously replied, with a rich smile, 'This is the first time I have ever been asked to do anything that was popular'. However, the *Daily News* felt that she was a popular enough figure to be reported. She had addressed a packed hall – there was not a seat to be had – on the subject of inequality in the employment of women and the reporter said that 'it was the most interesting paper read anywhere today', describing Lydia as

> . . . a hard hitter; but her missiles are facts; and it is only occasionally that she drops, in her quiet, telling way, a sarcasm with a bitter, keen edge to it.[68]

She enjoyed those sectional meetings which gave her an opportunity to pursue her favourite scientific interests. After the Birmingham congress she spent a happy week on a British Association field trip to Shropshire. The party travelled by train and were met by carriages at various stations along the line to be conveyed to sites of geological interest at Caradoc, the Long Mynd, the Stiperstones and Hope Bowdler where they studied fossils, and lastly to the historic Stokesay Castle. In 1884 she took the only extended holiday she had ever allowed herself and sailed for Montreal where the British Association was meeting, afterwards spending a few weeks with relatives who had settled in Canada. Even so, she undertook a series of articles for the *Manchester Examiner and Times* which helped to offset the cost of the trip.

Early in 1888 Lydia's colleagues began to observe with some alarm the she was losing her strength and vigour. She had always been susceptible to sudden nervous collapse after any specially anxious or strenuous effort but, alarming as these attacks always were at the time, they never came during a special campaign but always as a reaction after the event. She would normally recover quickly to fight another day but eventually the prolonged stress and anxiety began to tell upon her permanently. Throughout the winter of 1889–90 she was almost entirely confined to her house, 155 Shrewsbury Street, Manchester, where she had lived since her father died in 1877. Here she had a little conservatory which was her constant delight. Her flowering plants gave her immense pleasure just as, in the midst of the anxieties of her political work in London, she found relaxation and refreshment in Kew Gardens. Now she could no longer travel to London but she continued to work from home, mainly editing the *Women's Suffrage Journal*, but she felt lonely and isolated away from her office and welcomed the company of friends who broke the tedium of her enforced seclusion and helped her while away many weary hours with her favourite game of chess.

Early in 1890, with no improvement in her condition, Lydia set out for Bath in the hope that the milder climate and curative power of the waters might bring relief. She arranged for Helen Blackburn to deputise as editor of the *Women's Suffrage Journal* and, on arrival at her lodgings at 8 Queen Square in Bath, she wrote to her friends at the Central Committee in London:

> It is with great regret that I have to report the serious indisposition that disables me from attending at the office and from active work of all kinds. I am suffering from what the doctors call *rheumatoid arthritis* or *osteoarthritis* which cripples my limbs and undermines my strength. My physician says he can give me no hope of effective cure, but he advises me to devote a year to measures for the restoration of my health as far as it can be effected. He thinks I might return home for a while in a few weeks but of course nothing can be settled until it is seen how the cure progresses here. Since I have been here I have had the letters forwarded as usual so that the correspondence has gone on much the same as under ordinary circumstances when I am in London. It is not detrimental to me to continue this work – quite the contrary, as the post is something to work at day by day and my health and spirits would suffer if I were deprived altogether of my usual interests and occupations.[69]

The letter is long and she must have had considerable difficulty in writing it. At times her normally firm handwriting deteriorated into an almost illegible scrawl, but she felt duty bound to expound at some length on her concern about the financial position of the Society, her worries about parliamentary progress and the urgent need to summon a meeting of the Central Committee to receive the report of the Parliamentary Committee and to determine policy.

Her letters from Bath were cheerful and, although her physician, Dr Spender, could offer no dramatic cure, she did improve sufficiently to plan a further course of spa treatment at Aix les Bains. She set off in early summer, staying in London for a few days en route to take leave of her friends. On the day of her departure she even attended a meeting of the Committee in Great College Street on her way to Waterloo Station, so determined was she not to neglect her responsibilities. It was a formidable journey for someone in her crippled state; she was accompanied only by her maid but, with immense courage, made light of all the difficulties they encountered, but it seemed that, after a few weeks in Aix les Bains, she began to feel some benefit from the curative powers of the waters and, gradually, she began to walk again. Her letters began to sound more optimistic – she wrote of excursions to the lake and of her enjoyment of mountain drives. As strength returned she began once again to plan ahead and decided to take a trip into the French Alps. She was still writing regularly to Helen Blackburn and, in a letter dated 6th July, she described her arrival in St Gervais-les-Bains:

> Just arrived here and find your welcome letter and budget of newspapers, which I regard as a famished lion might look at a bone, after having had no news for some days. You must have thought I was lost, and so indeed I have been for the last two days – stuck in the bottom of a deep, damp hole from which escape seemed hard. I left Annecy on Thursday, *en route* for this place, which is reached by a cross-country railway, which strikes the beaten track from Geneva to Chamounix [sic] at a place called La Roche; the train passes up the wide valley of the Arne as far as Cluse, where the rail ends. The valley here contracts to a ravine, up which the diligence proceeds to Chamounix. The day was glorious and the country magnificent. When the diligence stopped at the point for St Gervais, I found that the village was three or four miles off, and I had not arranged for a conveyance, – so I was, perforce, obliged to stay the night at the Baths, which are situated at the bottom of a very

narrow, wooded ravine with perpendicular sides. There is just room for the buildings and the torrent. The place struck a damp chill into my very bones, and I made up my mind to get away next day; but there set in such a perfect torrent of unintermittent rain that I had not the courage to stir out; and only this afternoon have I escaped, and am rejoicing in re-entering the world again and rejoicing in the open air. This little place is truly enchanting and the air is like champagne . . .[70]

Subsequent letters seemed calculated to allay any fears about her health. She found the air invigorating and was planning to move on to Chamonix. She was still constantly working on suffrage matters, considering enlarging the work of the Central Committee and trying to decide whether she should leave Manchester and settle permanently in London where the campaign needed to be concentrated. On 15th July she sent Helen Blackburn instructions regarding a report on the annual meeting of the Central Committee which was to appear in the August number of the *Journal* and it was mentioned only in passing that she had been troubled with a severe throat infection for several days, unable to speak or take solid food. There was no doctor where she was staying and she was being treated by the local pharmacist. She had the company in the hotel of two kindly English ladies, a mother and daughter, who took her under their wing and kept an eye upon her. She hated being a prisoner in her room, looking out upon glorious scenery now bathed in sunshine but unable to enjoy it but she wrote stoically of the need for 'patience and perseverance'. Two days later she wrote again giving careful, precise instructions regarding the proofs of the issue of the *Journal* then in preparation but, to the consternation of her friends at home, the letter continued:

My illness has been very serious and I am afraid to think what might have happened if there had not been skilled medical attendance at hand. The *pharmacien* here has a diploma for medical practice, and has had eight years'

practice in Algeria. He has visited me three times a day to attend to the throat. To-day he brought in Dr Bonnafoy of Sallanches, who has been twice and increased the vigour of the remedies. Both doctors pronounce me decidedly better, as indeed I feel, and they expect that in two days I shall be convalescent and able to take solid food. My experience of the French doctors is very satisfactory; they are so very capable and skilful. I must, of course, stay on here till I am quite restored, so please continue to send things. Papers of all sorts will be doubly welcome while I am such a close prisoner in my small room.[71]

In spite of the lucidity of her letter she had been much troubled by nightmares and was obviously in considerable pain and, only a few hours after writing it her doctor perceived a change for the worse and gave his opinion that her only hope lay in the greater skill of a specialist doctor in Geneva. Diphtheria had been diagnosed and Lydia, with typical courage and stoicism, decided to make the forty mile journey but first she telegraphed the address of the Geneva doctor to her brothers and begged them to come to her because she was so desperately ill. She set out with only her personal maid in attendance; it was a beautiful day and the air seemed to brace her up, but she looked at her watch with some apprehension and wrote – because she could not speak – 'I shall not live to get there'. She did, in fact, reach Geneva, but it was only to find that the doctor to whom she had an introduction was not at home, and they spent a further gruelling two hours searching for someone to take her in. She was eventually admitted to the Clinique Juillard where she was given the best attention, but by now she was beyond help. Sitting in a chair waiting for the doctor to arrive she asked for some tea and, immediately after taking it, she died. Her brothers had been unable to reach her in time and it was a lonely death, far from family and friends. She was buried in the beautiful cemetery of St George in Geneva on Monday, 21st July 1890.

Chapter 10

WHEN the news of Lydia's death reached England the suffrage movement was stunned. A few weeks before setting out for France she had said that 'the movement has got far beyond depending on any individual' yet, however strong the determination of the suffrage societies, the loss of her guiding force was a devastating setback. The Manchester Committee was for a time like a body paralysed, the Central Committee suffered grievously without her political acumen and detailed knowledge of parliamentary procedure and the *Women's Suffrage Journal* simply ceased to exist.

To suffragists everywhere, to Members of Parliament and to the general public, Lydia Becker had been the visible hand of the movement. She had lifted the whole question of women's rights clear of the general atmosphere of shallow and flippant mockery which was prevalent in the early days of her campaign and into the realm of serious debate. With great courage and energy she had contended with the prejudice of generations and, although it was not given her to see the fruits of her labours, she did live long enough to see many of the old prejudices swept away and replaced by ideas of greater tolerance and freedom.

She was widely respected for her grasp of public affairs and admired for her clarity of expression, organisational ability and boundless enthusiasm, yet it became increasingly apparent over the years that her strategy of seeking to influence back-benchers and of encouraging private members' bills was doomed to failure without the open support of either party leader. Gladstone had made known his 'deep and sincere hatred' of the 1832 Reform Bill. He did not believe that popular representation was desirable, even for men, and thought that

> . . . it ought to be fixed, for the sake of the people themselves, at the minimum point consistent with infusing such a portion of public feeling into the legislature as shall effectively prevent oppression.[72]

He argued against female suffrage on the grounds that it would 'trespass upon the delicacy, the purity, the refinement' of women's nature, but he was deeply concerned that women were more likely to vote Tory and put him out of office and that, by enfranchising them, the way was open for women to become Members of Parliament and, even more unthinkable, be eligible for every high office of the State. So, although in principle many Liberals supported the women's cause, in practice their loyalty to their leader took precedence over personal conviction. Rank and file Conservatives, on the other hand, were generally opposed to the whole idea of giving the vote to women, although Disraeli had voted for the Women's Disabilities Removal Bill in 1871 and, two years later, had written to Mr Gore–Langton MP:

> As I believe this anomaly to be injurious to the best interests of the country, I trust to see it removed by the wisdom of Parliament.[73]

Despite these sentiments he did not use his influence when it could have been most effective, namely when he was Prime Minister, but he was then cultivating close and cordial relations with the Queen whose opposition to women's rights was well known. Sir Thomas Biddulph, keeper of her privy purse, thought that 'Dizzy is a perfect slave to the Queen' and it was unlikely that Disraeli would place that favoured relationship in jeopardy.

It was a cruel quirk of fate that, throughout Lydia's campaigning years, the suffragists had faced either a Conservative leader who claimed to favour their cause but with a rank and file who were vehemently opposed, or a hostile Liberal Prime Minister whose rank and file were, by and large, sympathetic, a situation which created deadlock in both camps. But, although Lydia did not live to see the franchise extended to women, it could never be argued that she had worn herself out in a lost cause. She had raised the consciousness of women, brought them together in their thousands to demand a greater degree of freedom and independence and she had shown them their potential strength. She had seen other laws passed which acknowledged women's rights and she had been enabled to fulfil a pioneering role in local government.

In the years immediately following her death there was an inevitable mood of despondency and inaction in the suffrage movement but new impetus came in the mid-nineties with the granting of the franchise to women in New Zealand and South Australia, and by the large numbers of members returned to Parliament in 1895 who had, in their election manifestoes at least, pledged support to The Cause. Towards the end of the century women textile workers in the north of England had joined the movement in large numbers when the question of a political levy was being discussed by the trade unions and they were encouraged by Lydia's Manchester Suffrage Society whose secretary was then Eva Gore–Booth with Mrs Emmeline Pankhurst a prominent member.[74]

Lydia's style had been essentially one of quiet, steady propaganda, working always by constitutional means; she believed that water dripping on a stone ultimately had an effect and her methods succeeded in placing women's suffrage constantly on the political agenda. Emmeline Pankhurst, on the other hand, a much younger and more flamboyant woman, lost patience with the methods of the Manchester Society, which she thought old-fashioned and tiresome, and broke away to initiate her own suffrage society, the Women's Social and Political Union, which subsequently earned such notoriety as to eclipse all the years of painstaking effort which had preceded it and helped to make it possible.

It was ironic that the final breakthrough came at a time when all suffrage agitation was in abeyance for the duration of the First World War, but in the end it was the war that created the right climate of public opinion for an idea 'whose time had come'. Women had made a vital contribution to the war effort and proved their indispensable value to the industrial and economic life of the nation. Leaders of the suffrage campaign were in the forefront of war work, using their ready-made network and organisational skills to alleviate suffering and hardship. There was a coalition government in office under pro-suffragist Lloyd George and, when the Representation of the People Bill was introduced in 1917 the Prime Minister and the leaders of every party supported the clause to include women in its provisions and, on 6th February 1918, it became the law of the land.

Twenty-eight years after Lydia's death the first women cast their votes, but only those above the age of thirty were allowed to do so. A further ten years were to pass before Lydia's dream was realised and women were given the vote on the same terms as men. The year was 1928, sixty-two years after Lydia's crusade had begun.

Notes and References

1. Sir Theodore Martin (1816–1909), official biographer of Albert, Prince Consort, quotes the Queen in his book *Queen Victoria as I knew her* (Blackwood, 1908).

2. Ludwig Mond (1839–1909) made his home in Britain in 1867 and established many industrial chemical processes to meet the demands of the expanding textile industry. The Brunner family settled in Liverpool from Switzerland in 1832 and John Brunner (1842–1919) entered into partnership with Mond to set up the largest alkali works in the world at Northwich. He endowed many schools and libraries and became an MP in the 1890s.

3. John Bright (1811–1889) came of Quaker stock and was an active member of the Anti-Corn Law League. He was a Radical Liberal MP for Durham (1843–1847), Manchester (1847–1857) and Birmingham (1857–1889) and President of the Board of Trade (1868–1870).

4. Esther Becker's notebook is deposited with the Becker papers in the Fawcett Library, Box 448.

5. Hermann Piutti's letter is reproduced in *Blackburn*, pp. 26–27.

6. Louis Philippe (1773–1850), king of France 1830–1848 but fled to England when the barricades went up in Paris following his ban on a meeting for franchise reform. He died at Claremont in Surrey.

7. Charles Darwin (1809–1882), famous naturalist and scientific writer and author of *Origin of Species* (1859).

8. Jessie Boucherett (1825–1905) founded the Society for Promoting the Employment of Women; together with Barbara Bodichon and Emily Davies drafted the petition which John Stuart Mill took to Parliament in 1866. Revived the feminist periodical *Englishwoman's Review* and was its editor until 1871.

9. *Stargazing for Novices* is deposited with the Becker papers in the Fawcett Library, Box 448.

10. Johann Friedrich Schiller, 18th-century German poet and dramatist, published his *Wallenstein* trilogy in 1798/9, a powerful tragedy in Greek style of a great man's struggle against forces that are too strong for him.

11. The complete text of the address, given on 30th January 1867, is reproduced in *Blackburn*, pp. 31–39.

12. Barbara Leigh Smith Bodichon (1827–1891) was largely responsible for the foundation of the first Women's Suffrage Committee in 1866. After her marriage to Frenchman Eugene Bodichon in 1857 she divided her time between Algeria and England. There is a biography of Barbara Bodichon by Hester Burton (John Murray, 1949).

13. *Reasons for the enfranchisement of women* was published as a pamphlet by the Social Science Association in 1866 and is available at the Fawcett Library.

14. Florence Nightingale (1820–1910) became a popular heroine after she took a group of nurses to the Crimea in 1854 and she subsequently campaigned tirelessly for improvements in army conditions. Harriet Martineau (1802–1876) was particularly involved in the controversy over the Contagious Diseases Acts. An invalid for most of her life, her most important contribution to feminism was through her writing. Louisa Twining (1820–1911), daughter of Richard Twining, head of the tea firm, was drawn into the women's movement by her concern at appalling conditions in workhouses and her efforts to involve women in workhouse administration and visiting.

15. John Stuart Mill (1806–1873), political economist and philosopher, with a firm belief in the equality of the sexes. Published his essays *On Liberty* and *The Subjection of Women* in 1869.

16. Josephine Butler (1828–1906), a convinced feminist but never very active in the suffrage campaign, her chief work being in the repeal of the Contagious Diseases Acts and her courage in bringing into the open the whole question of sexual immorality. Mary Somerville (1780–1872) was one of the foremost women of science in 19th century. The public recognition given to

her scientific writings helped to advance the cause of women's education and emancipation.

17. Emily Davies pioneered the admission of women to higher education and the professions on the same terms as men. Founded a women's college outside Cambridge in 1869 which became Girton College in 1873. Elizabeth Garrett Anderson (1836–1917), the first woman doctor. She sat the examinations of the Society of Apothecaries in 1865 and set up in practice in London. She married James Skelton Anderson in 1871. Sister of Millicent Fawcett.

18. Henry Alford (1810–1871), Dean of Canterbury from 1857 until his death and first editor of the *Contemporary Review*.

19. Jacob Bright (1821–1899) entered Parliament as MP for Manchester in 1867 and became leader of the suffragists in Parliament after John Stuart Mill lost his seat in 1868, until he too lost his seat in 1874. Introduced the first women's suffrage bill in 1870. Brother of John Bright, also a radical, but not a supporter of the suffrage campaign.

20. Female Suffrage by Lydia Becker in *Contemporary Review*, March 1867, v. 4, pp. 307–316.

21. Manchester Archives, Letters to Lydia Becker, M50/1/2/1–65, box 1.

22. *Hansard's Parliamentary Debates*, 3rd series, v.187, c817–c845.

23. Alexander Beresford-Hope (1820–1887), MP for Maidstone intermittently between 1841 and 1848 and Cambridge University MP 1868–1887. Anti-suffrage speech in House of Commons, 3rd May 1871, reproduced in *Women in Public 1850–1900* (Hollis), pp. 304–305.

24. Blackburn, *Women's Suffrage*, p. 65.

25. Letter to an unknown correspondent, quoted by Blackburn, op. cit., p. 68.

26. Richard Marsden Pankhurst (1835–1898) was called to the bar in 1867 and became an executive member of the Manchester Suffrage Society. He drafted the Women's Disabilities Removal Bill of 1870 and Jacob Bright's amendment to the Municipal Corporations Bill of 1869. He married Emmeline Goulden in 1879.

27. Thomas Chisholm Anstey (1816–1873) was called to the bar in 1839 and first returned to Parliament as a Liberal in 1847. Professor of law and jurisprudence and attorney-general in Hong Kong 1855–1859. His paper *On some supposed constitutional restraints on the parliamentary*

franchise was published by the Social Science Association (1867) and is among the bound volumes of pamphlets in the Fawcett Library.

28. Lord Henry Brougham (1778–1868), held offices of Attorney–General and Lord Chancellor, president of the Social Science Association 1857 and 1860–65. Active in the cause of law reform. His Interpretation Act was passed in 1850 (13 and 14 Vict., c21, section 4).

29. Henry Davis Pochin (1824–1895) was twice Mayor of Salford, 1866–1867 and 1867–1868, before becoming Liberal MP for Stafford in 1868. In 1866 he published *A Plan of Parliamentary Reform* advocating the claims of the working classes. His wife, Agnes, who moved the second resolution at the Manchester meeting had published a pamphlet in 1855, three years after her marriage, under the name Justitia, *The Right of Women to Exercise the Elective Franchise*. Manchester Women's Suffrage Society re-issued it in 1873. The resolutions are quoted in Blackburn, *Women's Suffrage*, pp. 71–72.

30. Letter book of Lydia Becker, no. 150. Manchester Archives, M50/1/3.

31. Sir John Coleridge (1821–1894), was made Queen's Counsel in 1861 and was Solicitor-General 1868–1871, when he became Attorney-General. A decided Liberal, in favour of a much larger distribution of Parliamentary seats. Lord Chief Justice of Common Pleas, 1873 and Lord Chief Justice of England 1880–1894.

32. Russell Gurney (1804–1878), Queen's Counsel 1845 and Recorder of London 1856 and Conservative MP for Southampton 1865–1878.

33. Ursula Bright (1830–1915), leading equal rights feminist, particularly involved in campaigning for Married Women's Property Acts. Married Jacob Bright in 1855. Lydia was a regular visitor to their home at Alderley Edge.

34. Blackburn, op. cit., p. 90.

35. Letter Book of Lydia Becker, no. 291. Manchester Archives, M50/1/3.

36. Loc. cit., no. 323.

37. Loc. cit., no. 249.

38. Pankhurst, E. S., p. 41.

39. Letter Book of Lydia Becker, no. 414.

40. Anti-Suffrage Review, December 1908, p. 2.

41. *Hansard*, House of Lords, 19th July 1869, c145.

42. *Rights and duties of women in local government*, 1879.

43. Scrapbook of newspaper cuttings. Manchester Archives, BRf 324.3 B6.
44. Letter to Manchester Examiner and Times, 2nd April 1873.
45. Address to British Association, Edinburgh, 8 August 1871.
46. Helen Blackburn (1842–1903), worked with Central Committee of NWSS 1874–1895, editor of *Englishwoman's Review* 1881–1890. Author of *Women's Suffrage* (1902).
47. Elizabeth Wolstenholme Elmy (1834–1913), well known headmistress who set up the Manchester Schoolmistresses Association in 1865. Founder member of Manchester Women's Suffrage Committee and lived to be a prominent suffragette.
48. *Women's Suffrage Journal*, August 1873.
49. Charlotte Carmichael Stopes, passionate advocate of women's suffrage. Met Henry Stopes at a British Association meeting. Mother of Marie Stopes, birth control campaigner.
50. *Women's Suffrage Journal*, December 1889.
51. Loc. cit., July 1870.
52. Loc. cit., memorial number, August 1890.
53. Lady Anne Gore–Langton lived at Newton Park, between Bath and Bristol, and was active in both the Bath and Bristol Suffrage Societies. Her husband, William, Conservative MP for West Somerset, was responsible for presenting Disraeli with a Memorial signed by 11,000 women in support of female suffrage in April 1873.
54. Leonard Henry Courtney (1832–1918), journalist and statesman, described as one of the ablest and most advanced Liberals. Leader writer for *The Times*, 1865–1881. Fierce advocate of proportional representation.
55. Blackburn, *Women's Suffrage*, p. 143.
56. Priscilla Bright McLaren, president of the Edinburgh Women's Suffrage Society and wife, mother, sister and aunt of Members of Parliament. Blackburn said she had "the longest unbroken record of office of any worker of The Cause".
57. Letters to Lydia Becker. Manchester Archives, M50/1/2, box 1.
58. Lady Frances Verney was the sister of Florence Nightingale. Millicent Garrett Fawcett (1847–1929) was the younger sister of Elizabeth Garrett Anderson. She joined the London Suffrage Committee in 1867, slowly emerging as one of the leaders of the movement in 1880s. She took over the leadership of the National Union of Women's Suffrage Societies on Lydia's death and held the position until 1919, but she never allied herself with the militant tactics of the suffragettes.
59. Sophia Jex-Blake (1840–1912), pioneer in the medical education of women. Qualified as a doctor in Dublin in 1877, set up a successful practice in Edinburgh and founded her own medical school for women.
60. *The Times*, 21st May 1884.
61. William Woodall (1832–1901), Liberal MP for Stoke on Trent (1880–1885) and Hanley (1885–1900). Owned a china business in Burslem and was chairman of Burslem School Board. Introduced women's suffrage bills in 1884, 1889 and 1891.
62. *Hansard's Parliamentary Debates*, 3rd series, v.288, c1958–9.
63. Frances Power Cobbe (1822–1904), journalist and anti-vivisectionist. Her chief contribution to feminism was through her writings, particularly on male violence.
64. *Women's Suffrage Journal*, August 1877, pp. 90–91.
65. Loc. cit., July 1877, p. 77.
66. Loc. cit., August 1877, p. 91.
67. Loc. cit., memorial number, August 1890, p. 4.
68. *Daily News*, 9th August 1871.
69. Filed among Letters to Lydia Becker, Manchester Archives M50/1/2, box 2.
70. Blackburn: *Women's Suffrage*, pp. 182–183.
71. Op. cit., pp. 184–185.
72. W. E. Gladstone. The Prime Minister's papers: II Autobiographical memoranda. HMSO, 1972.
73. Letter dated 29 April 1873 and published in Englishwoman's Review, July 1873, p. 218.
74. Eva Gore–Booth (1870–1926), joint secretary with Esther Roper of the Women's Textile and Other Workers' Representation Committee in Manchester, 1897, and an active campaigner to bring women's suffrage to working women. Emmeline Pankhurst (1858–1928) worked for women's suffrage in Manchester until 1885 when she and husband Richard, 24 years her elder, moved to London. She founded the Women's Social and Political Union (suffragettes) in 1903.

Bibliography

Banks, O. *Biographical dictionary of British feminists*, v.1 1800–1930. Wheatsheaf Books, 1985.

Becker, L. E. *Botany for novices: a short outline of the natural system of classification of plants*, London, Whittaker, 1864, viii + 60pp.

Becker, L. E. *The equality of women: a paper read before the British Association at Norwich*, 1868.

Becker, L. E. 'Female suffrage', *Contemporary Review*, 1867, v.4., pp. 307–316.

Becker, L. E. *Liberty, equality, fraternity: a reply to Mr FitzJames Stephen's strictures on Mr J. S. Mill's Subjection of women*, Manchester, 1874, 27pp.

Becker, L. E. 'On the study of science by women', *Contemporary Review*, 1869, v. 10, pp. 386–404.

Becker, L. E. 'The political disabilities of women', *Westminster Review*, 1872, new series v. 41, pp. 50–70.

Becker, L. E. A reply to the protest (against the extension of the parliamentary franchise to women) which appeared in the *Nineteenth Century Review*, June 1889 . . . Reprinted by permission from the *Manchester Guardian*. Manchester, *Women's Suffrage Journal*, 1889.

Becker, L. E. *The rights and duties of women in local government*, Manchester, A. Ireland and Co., 1879, 11pp.

Becker, L. E. *Women's suffrage: substance of a lecture*, 1869, 16pp.

Blackburn, H. *Women's suffrage: a record of the women's suffrage movement in the British Isles, with biographical sketches of Miss Becker*, London and Oxford, Williams and Norgate, 1902, x + 298pp.

Blackburn, H. *Words of a leader: being extracts from the writings of the late Miss Lydia Becker*, Bristol, J. W. Arrowsmith, 1897, 41pp.

Blake, R. *Disraeli*. Methuen, 1966.

Bodichon, B. *Reasons for the enfranchisement of women*, London, Social Science Association, 1866, 12pp.

Dolton, C. B. 'The Manchester School Board', thesis for part 2 of the degree of Master of Education at the University of Durham. Durham, 1959.

Fulford, R. *Votes for women: the story of a struggle*, London, Faber, 1957, 343pp.

Gladstone, W. E. *Female suffrage. A letter to Samuel Smith MP*, John Murray, 1892.

Gladstone, W. E. *The Prime Minister's papers. II Autobiographical memoranda*, HMSO, 1972.

Hansards Parliamentary Debates. 3rd series, v. 187 onwards. Cornelius Buck, 1867 onwards.

Hill, C. P., *British economic and social history 1700–1982*, 5th ed. Hodder and Stoughton, 1985.

Holcombe, L. *Victorian ladies at work: middle-class working women in England and Wales 1850–1914*, David and Charles, 1973.

Hollis, P. *Ladies elect: women in English local government 1865–1914*, OUP, 1987.

Hollis, P. *Women in public 1850–1900: documents of the Victorian women's movement*, London, Allen and Unwin, 1979.

Holmes, M. *Lydia Becker: a cameo life-sketch*, London, Women's Freedom League, 2nd edition, 1913, 29pp.

Liddington, J. and Norris, J. *One hand tied behind us: the rise of the women's suffrage movement*, London, Virago, 1978, 304pp.

Manchester National Society for Women's Suffrage. *Annual Reports* 1868–1890.

Manchester School Board. *Reports 1871–1900*.

Mill, J. S. *The subjection of women*, 2nd edition, 1869, 188pp.

Pankhurst, E. S. *The Suffragette movement*, London, Longman 1931, reprinted Virago, 1977.

Pankhurst, R. 'The right of women to vote under the Reform Act of 1867', *Fortnightly Review*, September 1868.

Read, D. *England 1868–1914*, London, Longman, 1979.

Rosen, A. *Rise up women!* London, Routledge and Kegan Paul, 1974.

Rover, C. *Women's suffrage and party politics in Britain 1866–1914*, Routledge and Kegan Paul, 1967.

Shepherd, F. M. *Lydia Becker: some biographical notes*. Typescript, 1977.

Spender, D. ed. *Education papers: women's quest for equality in Britain 1850–1912*, London, Routledge and Kegan Paul, 1987 (Women's Source Library).

Stancliffe, F. S. *John Shaw's 1738–1938*, Sherratt and Hughes, 1938, 424pp.

Stenton, M. *Who's who of British Members of Parliament*, v. 1 1832–1885 and v. 2 1886–1918. Harvester Press, 1976 and 1978.

Strachey, R. *The Cause*, London, G. Bell and sons, 1928, reprinted Virago, 1978.

Women's Suffrage Journal 1870–1890, edited by Lydia E. Becker, 1870–1890.

Miscellaneous papers deposited in Manchester Central Library, Archives Department and Local History Library and in the Fawcett Library, City of London Polytechnic.

Occasional Papers from the Centre for North-West Regional Studies

Flowering Plants and Ferns of Cumbria	G. Halliday	£2.95
Early Lancaster Friends	M. Mullet	£2.95
North-West Theses and Dissertations, 1950–78	U. Lawler	£6.00
Lancaster: The Evolution of its Townscape to 1800	S. Penney	£2.95
Richard Marsden and the Preston Chartists, 1837–48	J. King	£2.95
The Grand Theatre, Lancaster	A. Betjemann	£2.95
Popular Leisure and the Music Hall in 19th-century Bolton	R. Poole	£2.95
Industrial Archaeology of the Lune Valley	J. Price	£2.95
The Diary of William Fisher of Barrow, 1811–59	W. Rollinson/B. Harrison	£2.95
Rural Life in South-West Lancashire, 1840–1914	A. Mutch	£3.95
Grand Fashionable Nights: Kendal Theatre, 1575–1985	M. Eddershaw	£3.95
The Roman Fort and Town of Lancaster	D. Shotter/A. White	£4.95
Windermere in the nineteenth century	O. M. Westall	£4.95
A Traditional Grocer: T. D. Smith's of Lancaster	M. Winstanley	£4.95
Reginald Farrer: Dalesman, Planthunter, Gardener	J. Illingworth/J. Routh	£4.95
Walking Roman Roads in Bowland	P. Graystone	£4.95
The Royal Albert: Chronicles of an Era	J. Alston	£4.95
From Lancaster to the Lakes – The Region in Literature	K. Hanley/A. Milbank	£5.95
The Buidings of Georgian Lancaster	A. White	£5.95

Each of these titles may be ordered by post from:

**C.N.W.R.S.,
Fylde College,
University of Lancaster,
Bailrigg, Lancaster**

**Books will be despatched post free to UK addresees.
Please make cheques payable to 'The University of Lancaster'.
Titles are also available from all good booksellers within the region.**